Past Life & Spirit World Regressions

Healing Through Revealing Soul

Shannon Peck

Past Life & Spirit World Regression

Healing through Revealing Soul

First Edition, Copyright © 2020 by Shannon Peck

Update 5

Lifepath Publishing

1127 Santa Luisa, Solana Beach, CA 92075

All rights reserved. Printed in the United States of America. No part of this book may be reproduced or transmitted in any form or by any means, electronic or mechanical, including photocopying, recording, or by any information storage and retrieval system without written permission from the author, except for the inclusion of quotations in a review.

Cover art by Daniel Holeman: AwakenVisions.com

Cover by Killer Covers

Printed by Amazon Kindle Print

ISBN-13: 9781657843387

ISBN-10: 1657843386

Disclaimer: The information contained in this book is not intended as medical advice. The author, publisher, and distributor do not assume responsibility for any adverse consequences resulting from adopting the ideas in this book. It is the hope of the author that, one day, we will no longer need to disclaim information vital to our health, healing, and spiritual progress.

Also by Shannon Peck

Love Heals
How to Heal Everything with Love

Love Heals Study Guide
Designed for individual & group study

Soul Mate Love
Inside Secrets from an Authentic Soul Mate Couple

Co-authored with Scott Peck

The Love You Deserve
A Spiritual Guide to Genuine Love

Co-authored with Scott Peck

Love Skills You Were Never Taught
Secrets of a Love Master

Co-authored with Scott Peck

Liberating Your Magnificence
Opening Your Life to Infinite Possibilities

Co-authored with Scott Peck

Acknowledgments

Little did I know at the time I began writing this book that it would bring such a powerful transformation into my life.

As the book process gained momentum, it pulled me into a vast expansion propelling my soul's growth, which has been a wonderful surprise and it also changed me. There are 3 key people who I want to thank profusely.

I wish to express the wonderful fortune of being trained as a Past Life Regression counselor by Dr. Linda Backman. You will read more about Linda in the Introduction. My heart pours out with gratitude and admiration having her as a role model and influence on the subject of regression and the soul. And I'll tell you why.

Linda is renowned for being one of the world's most knowledgeable regression therapists, having given in excess of an astounding 10,000 regressions over a period of the last 24 years. I love calling her for her updates as she is constantly learning, as I am, from her guides, about souls. Her many years of experience have taught her volumes on this all important subject. She is truly an authority and expert on the subject.

Linda treats her clients with great tenderness, respect, and sacredness. She truly honors her clients as souls. Because of her loving influence and teachings, I am able to offer professional Past Life and Spirit World

Regressions as a spiritual healer. This is my life passion.

I wish to also thank my beloved husband and soul mate, Scotty, who has been lovingly by my side cheering me on from the very beginning when this book was just a small idea in the back of my mind.

His confidence and encouragement were a powerful ignition and inspiration launching me into action. And his constant interest and discussions about the subject of past life regression as well as the book's content, helped to shape this book. These contributions have taken me to a new level as a regressionist. Through his love and belief in me, I was able to write this book so important to my soul.

As the book gathered steam and I began writing about the regressions which I was giving, I realized that I needed a sharp editor to help keep me on track. Then something wonderful happened. My guides sent the finest editor in the world to come and help me, my daughter, Kaia Alexander.

Through our many months together pouring over the magnificent regressions, her intelligent questions continually lifted me higher and caused me to clarify my role and skills as a regressionist while she assisted me with clarity, so important for each regression's story.

From her high standard of requiring refined explanations and definitions, I found my clear voice to describe what happened in the regressions, the benefits, and how it changed my clients. It's been a wonderful gift being able to work together and getting closer as mother-daughter.

This has all been to serve the goal of showing you the endless possibilities of Past Life and Spirit World Regressions. I hope that you find it as fascinating and educational as I do!

Contents

Books by Shannon Peck

Acknowledgments

Contents

Introduction ... 11

Part I

Chapter 1: Your Soul ... 21

Chapter 2: Past Life Regression ... 37

Chapter 3: Spirit World Regression ... 55

Part II – Past Life Regression Stories

Chapter 4: Clearing Blocks of Sadness and Depression ... 73

Chapter 5: Healing Childhood Trauma and Reuniting with God's Presence ... 81

Chapter 6: Lean on Your Guides and Know You Are Not Alone ... 89

Chapter 7: Love is What You Came Here to Learn and Protect ... 103

Chapter 8: Overcoming Grief and Reconnecting with a Deceased Loved One ... 113

Chapter 9: Self-Worth and Life Purpose Realized ... 129

Part III – Spirit World Regression Stories

Chapter 10: A Destiny with Prosperity ... 141

Chapter 11: An Interplanetary Soul and A Spirit Guide in Training ... 157

Chapter 12: A Light Worker from the Angelic Realm ... 169

Chapter 13: A Soul of Infinite Possibilities ... 181

Chapter 14: Strength and Protection from Archangel Michael ... 191

Chapter 15: My Own Personal Regressions ... 201

About the Author

How to Contact or Book a Session

Introduction

I've been a spiritual healer for over 35 years.

My spiritual service began in the mid 1970s when I was first guided to become a professional spiritual healer. In response to a feeling of great compassion for others, I developed a private healing practice, offering healing through metaphysics, prayer, and intuition. I answered calls for help on a daily basis, offering my love while giving the finest healing response, based on divine guidance, that I could possibly offer my clients.

I witnessed a world of endless and wonderful - even miraculous - healings. Some were physical, some were emotional, and many were life changing. I found that transformation through divine guidance brought immense liberation to my clients.

Over the years, I became increasingly aware of the power of love to bring healing, whether the problem was a health problem, a troubling relationship, financial distress, a life crisis, or other challenge.

Sometimes healings came easily and swiftly but, at other times, there seemed to be hidden problems presenting complexities which were controlling the situation. I learned how to use intuition and prayer to uncover many of the greater, hidden problems which required attention in order to actualize the healing.

Often, I found that an emotional crisis or trauma from troubling relationships manifested as a disease, an illness, or another physical condition. At these times, I always dug deeper to try and uncover the hidden layers of the original problem. I agree with recovery expert Gabor Mate when he says, "The issues are in the tissues."

In the mid 1990s I came across a book, Journey of Souls by Dr. Michael Newton, where he shared his story as a therapist who accidentally discovered that his client had not only gone back to a past life but that she was in another place entirely.

He came to understand that she had gone to Spirit World, a home base for the soul and where we go in between lives. I was fascinated and wanted to learn more, yet the subject was new and little was known about it. Few books existed on the subject.

Even today, information about this all-important subject is relatively new to the past few decades and spiritual seekers like me and my clients who want more because the subject is so powerfully transforming, awakening, and healing. That's also why I'm writing this book.

Also, as I delve into how other regressionists like myself are doing the work, I not only find their work to be greatly inspiring, but I'm discovering that each of us utilizes different techniques and approaches to regressions. There's much to gain from further research, publishing, and sharing. The possibilities open to us through Past Life and Spirit World Regressions are truly limitless!

My distinction is that I approach regression as a healer and, as a healer, I'm acutely aware of the transformative power of witnessing your Higher Self.

My many years of training have taught me that defining the answer to the question, "Who are you?" leads directly to an awakening to your soul which opens the door to a world of healing.

Around the year 2000, after decades of healing, I arrived at the conclusion that one of the factors that affects and even determines healing is self-love. Most people barely scratch the surface of loving themselves and it bears a great cost across lifetimes.

Another factor that affects and influences your ability - or inability - to heal is the love or lack of love shared in your most intimate relationships. I've come to the realization that these 2 factors combined would resolve a world of your problems and they also hold great potential for your happiness.

About this time, in addition to having a spiritual healing practice, my husband Scott Peck and I began writing books and articles on love.

Our work together then morphed into doing workshops on love and healing. We also hosted a live weekly national radio broadcast on SIRIUS satellite, called, "Love Talk," where we took questions from listeners and dived into the deep end, applying love and healing to people's relationships, while exploring solutions that bring deeper understanding.

In 2006 my parents moved to San Diego from Arkansas. My daughter gave birth to my grandson in 2011, and also moved nearby. These were happy but demanding years.

My parents who were energetic, happy, and mentally lucid required help as they entered their nineties, and so I became their caregiver until their deaths in 2016 and 2017 respectfully.

I feel so fortunate to have been there to give generous love and care to them until the end of their lives. During these years, I found it necessary to retire from my spiritual healing practice since I could no longer accommodate healing appointments in my schedule.

I'm grateful that I was able to care for each of my elderly parents all the way through their hospice care and death. This intense experience led me to read many books on death and dying.

During this time, I was contemplating the entire process of death and dying as well as the immortality of our souls.

Where do we go after dying? What do we do? My interest culminated with Past Life and Spirit World Regressions where I've discovered many answers to these major issues.

Plus, it's opened me and my clients to feeling deep comfort about the entire process of dying and what happens afterward, as there is no question the soul lives beyond death. This has become my life purpose and has shaped my attitude about living and dying.

In the midst of my caregiving years, in 2013, my daughter gave me a book about past life regression by Linda Backman, Ed.D.

Dr. Backman had worked with Michael Newton and been with the Newton Institute, personally co-developing the training program with Dr. Newton for their Between Lives Regression therapists.

I was intensely interested in meeting her and experiencing what she called a "Between Lives Soul Regression" (what I call in this book a Spirit World Regression). It felt like an extension from when I first learned about this subject from Michael Newton's book, Journey of Souls.

Linda was coming to California within a few weeks and I scheduled a regression with her. Little did I know back then that I was morphing into an entirely new method of healing, only this time it would be what I consider to be the zenith of all healing methods.

My regression with Linda was life changing as I saw the possibilities of who I am as a soul.

Soon after my regression with her, I learned that Linda was training her own students to become regression therapists. I leapt at the chance! My husband, Scott, joined me in the training and together we became certified Past Life and Between Lives Soul Regression counselors.

After our training and in coming years, we gave each other over 50 regressions to explore the topic thoroughly. And to this day, we still give each other regressions. As a result, our lives have changed dramatically.

We discovered that the Higher Self, your soul, is very real. And, beyond your personality, your soul is your true identity.

Because we came to know each other as a Higher Self, or soul, this took precedence in our relationship. We became two souls loving each other as souls. Trust me when I tell you the deepening of the love and intimacy between us, as a result of this, is indescribable and beautiful.

Giving and receiving so many regressions tapped into my love of healing and a desire to offer regressions professionally.

In my work, I offer two forms of regressions: Past Life Regression and Spirit World Regression.

Regressions lend tremendous mental clarity and immediate practical solutions to your life, including your soul's purpose and meaning. It occurs within an enormous overarching context which can be gained in no other way. This immortal perspective offers astounding spiritual insight.

This book is a compilation of regressions with some of my clients.

When I explained to them that I wanted to write a book on the subject, they were delighted to offer their regressions as examples of the possibilities that wait like hidden gold nuggets for you to discover. I'm indebted to each of them for participating in this book. Their names have been changed to honor the privacy of their identity.

I have a tremendous love for regression as a powerful healing method. A regression shifts the healing from originating from a personal healer and, instead, through a regressed state of mind, empowers you to access your own healing information directly.

Plus, it takes significantly less time. I schedule regressions during a single afternoon that deliver great spiritual insight and stand to change your self-perception where you understand yourself outside of time, seeing yourself as a soul, and accessing divine guidance - all which shift your entire world.

In the process, you gain answers to your life problems, even ones you didn't know which began eons ago and which you may still suffer from. It's remarkably liberating.

Most fascinating is that Past Life and Spirit World Regressions allow insight into what your soul has been doing over lifetimes, including your present lifetime. I can't think of a more exciting or empowering way to know yourself inside out.

Your soul has wisdom and purpose, which are accessible to you through the methods outlined in this book. You may find that as you read the regressions, memories of your own past lives may begin to emerge.

It's my joy and honor to be your guide and to open this subject for your further exploration, while you begin to discover your own purpose and access the deep healing wisdom and clarity that resides within you.

PART 1

Chapter 1

Your Soul

Your soul is infinite.

You will never die. The lessons you learn as a soul are carried with you from lifetime to lifetime. The theme through all of my healing experience and research in both Past Life Regressions and Spirit World Regressions is that your soul carries a purpose, whether or not you are aware of that purpose.

In fact, your soul is in charge of your life.

I see this repeated in each new session with entirely new clients and from all over the world. Soul transcends culture, religion, family background, and life story. I'm passionate about the infinite complexity of our souls that incarnate for particular reasons, perhaps a reason left unfinished, carried over from previous lifetimes.

What I know as a spiritual healer is that identifying your soul is the most powerful information you can ever gain about yourself. Only then can you integrate with your Higher Self and come into alignment and harmony with its true purpose. This creates the opportunity for maximum growth and empowerment for your present life.

Regressions are a profound portal of transformation and spiritual guidance. These experiences give you access to deep understanding and provide information that can only be explored through a regression, since this level of depth about yourself seldom surfaces to a conscious level.

Past Life and Spirit World Regressions are truly the Mother Lode of healing opportunities.

Your soul is on a larger path of divinity, reflecting your true nature in the human experience even in the midst of the obstacle course of life, which can often seem so difficult to navigate.

These challenges are just what your soul needs in order to grow! It's all about your evolution as a soul. Whether you're a newborn baby or a hundred years old, your soul is engaged on its path of purpose, and it has much to accomplish.

It's true that the human experience is often extremely painful and overwhelming, and we often feel as though we're all alone trying to survive emotionally and physically while comparing ourselves with others who seem to have a much easier life while we continue to struggle with our own.

One thing is for sure: everyone could use more help and support on the path. As a healer, the kind of help I've found that comes through Past Life and Spirit World Regressions is monumental and life changing.

Your soul is a reservoir for your healings, your dreams, power, potential, and even many of your feelings.

It turns out that *your soul is who you are*. It encompasses all time including all of your lives. It has a plan for your present life that integrates all that you've ever been and will become. Within your soul's blueprint is your complete fulfillment the same way that an acorn holds the entire oak tree inside it.

Within you resides the vast and beautiful identity of your eternal self, your Higher Self. Once it's known, all you want is for it to take over your life so your life displays evidence of who you really are, and what you value most.

Unfortunately, it's not only possible but common that people live their entire lives out of touch with their souls, their true selves. When soul doesn't find expression in their lives they wonder why they feel hollow, unfulfilled, or even trapped.

Our culture conditions us to seek fulfillment through status, money, relationships, positions of power, the acquisition of stuff and more stuff, youth and beauty, reputation, and even fame.

The truth is, none of that is who you are, and none of it can come with you when you die. The only way to define yourself in a liberated way is as a soul, and through the qualities of your soul. Otherwise you're doomed to feel good only when you have the things that society tells you that you need to have to be validated or legitimate.

Many people are shocked to discover that having these things doesn't deliver lasting happiness or meaning. If you dare to age, or lose your fortune, or experience a setback, you'll be miserable if your identity is locked up in those things.

On the spectrum of self-realization, the more you express your soul, and are attuned to your soul, the more natural energy is available to you, expressing itself as love, joy, vitality, prosperity and providing you a sense of empowerment that enables you to live your full potential.

There's a point at which, when you awaken to your soul self, things in your life start to change dramatically.

As it becomes your heart's desire to listen and be guided so that your soul can come forward in every possible way, your soul begins to awaken, and you start to feel fulfilled. At that grand junction, your life becomes defined as your soul rather than a human who has a soul. And that is precisely what you want.

Listening to your soul

Your soul speaks to you through your intuition.

You can access your intuition by becoming aware of distinguishing your own thoughts from thoughts that come to you through an inner knowing, which you may refer to as your gut or your inner voice.

As you pay attention to it and take action, it will guide and shape your life. Unfortunately, we often ignore it. But what happens when you begin to pay attention to your intuition more regularly can be astounding to carve out your life in wondrous ways that you may have never thought of yourself.

Intuition is the ability to understand something from a direct perception of truth with no need for conscious reasoning. It's the voice of your soul.

Have you ever had an intuition that you ignored and then later it came back confirming itself as something that was true and worthy of attention?

In your everyday life have you ever thought of a friend and then the friend called you soon after?

Have you ever just missed the freeway jam because you listened to a little voice within that caused you to delay leaving your home?

Ever crossed the street because someone on the sidewalk had bad energy?

These are important moments to pay attention, where the inner voice of intuition speaks.

What you don't want is to remain inattentive to your soul or, worse yet, to remain ignorant of your soul.

Your soul has all of your answers, all of them. It has a plan for your life, for every moment and every day, and even eternally.

As you tune in, you'll begin to learn this. And you'll find yourself almost falling over to accommodate your soul. You learn that you don't dare not listen to it or rationalize it away!

Regressions are a great way to encounter your soul. The experience can be extraordinary and uncommon, where you shift away from how you normally perceive yourself and into a very enlarged sense of who you are and the importance of your soul.

Your soul incarnates into the human realm with a body and life that has immediate physical and emotional needs for survival, support, safety, and security. And although these represent important human needs, your soul also has important needs to fulfill its purpose, learn lessons, and gain experiences for learning and helping others.

Wisdom of the soul is visible through qualities such as: compassion, love, caring, generosity, forgiveness, wisdom, integrity, and equanimity. Your choices and decisions can enhance or ruin your lives on Earth and determine your soul's success in this life and others.

I was never taught soul as my identity. Growing up in a Baptist church, I learned to regard my soul as distant and inactive until, eventually at my time of death, my soul would be the part of me that goes on to heaven. It was confusing and it also made my soul sound irrelevant to my present life until I died.

You may have been brought up in a family, culture or religion that disregarded the soul, or even suggested that your soul could be damned or saved.

In my experience as a regressionist, there is only love and support for us on the other side. Your guides and teachers are always available to support you on your soul's journey through life.

Soul guidance through intuition

The more active your intuition, the less stress in your life. The reason is that it's far easier to orient the direction of your life from your Higher Self.

Your Higher Self, or soul, brings the power of wisdom and intelligence in a more illuminated way than the limited human self can. It's capable of managing everything in your life in full detail. Checking in with your Higher Self through your intuition is key to your soul advancing.

I set up my day each morning by checking in with my Higher Self for a few minutes, acknowledging its divinity as my identity and remembering that it has a wonderful plan for me and all the universe. For the rest for the day, I try to align myself with it by continual inner inquiries of my heart such as:

- What do I do now? (for example, when making decisions, e.g. while choosing a movie or a restaurant, or whether or not to take a job, move, or marry this person. You can also do this check-in during a crisis.)
- Is this the way? (Once you make a choice, request a confirmation.)
- How should I go about doing this?
- How should I think about this?
- What should I say to this person in this situation?
- What would most help this other person in this circumstance? (By connecting to your Higher Self, this helps to give you emotional freedom rather than to add the concern to your pile of fears and anxieties.
- Please give me a sign. I'll look for it.
- Check in with God to stay close. This check- in reminds me that I'm not alone. I'm being guided. I'm so thankful!

I know that by living close to my Higher Self through inquiry, I'll have the best day possible in every way. This means I'll be guided in what I say and do, how I respond, decision making, and problem solving, as well as holding myself to express kindness to myself and others.

This is the way to live from your soul and lead your life with spiritual influence. It gives new meaning to living true to yourself. The latter is extremely important for your karma, which means that what you express also comes back to you.

As you develop this habit of living intuitively, there's an accumulation. Over months and years from having your soul preside over your life, you'll realize that your life turned out very differently than if you hadn't lived according to your soul. It will surprise you in wonderful ways.

The more you devote yourself to this practice, the better your life will be. I have never found any Past Life or Spirit World Regression to bring harm in any way – only healing.

Is your soul the same as your Higher Self?

Yes. I use these terms synonymously.

Is Higher Self the same as God?

Yes. It's your God Self. When I think of the ever-evolving soul, I think of it as divine, complete, whole, immortal, infinite, and originated from and forever inseparable from All That is.

Past Life Regression introduces you to yourself as a soul who has been evolving and learning over eons. The experience is powerful to place you in a new context of yourself.

When I think of a Supreme Being or Infinite Presence I'm immediately in a place of love, awe, and vastness. You may have words to describe this such as: God, Goddess, Divine Love, Creator, the Universe, the Tao, Allah, etc.

It's practically impossible to comprehend anything so great as Divine Love. I have many names and terms to describe it: God, Holy Spirit, Divine Glory, divine Love, Spirit, Creator, and All That Exists. All names and terms apply!

It stands to reason that whatever created everything also created you.

Our human senses don't fully comprehend the reality of God or All That Exists. However, when we reach higher, through our spiritual senses or intuition, we can connect and align ourselves with divinity.

Regarding your relationship with the divine, there's one thing I am sure - you and the Divine are inseparable. And another point - the divine is an ever-evolving state. And so are you.

Soul emotion

One of the most surprising things to clients who come for regressions is that they cry during the regression, often more than once, and sometimes with immense catharsis. I always keep a box of tissue on hand!

There's no question that your soul carries feelings. Often these feelings are immense and even mythic in scale. Rather than call them negative or positive, these soul feelings might be best explained with the analogy of music.

Music can convey opening, tenderness, inspiration, awe, hope, joy, love, expectations, energy, relief, and happiness. But it can also convey sorrow, fear, worry, agitation, anger, and disappointment.

Sometimes, during a past life when you weren't able to feel those feelings, you carry them on to a new life.

Sometimes the feelings are so vast, and restricted by either circumstance (war, death, famine, migration) or beliefs (religious or cultural), that you never had a chance to reconcile with them during that life or in between lives. Or you died so suddenly that there was no resolution.

During a regression, some of these feelings will surface, sometimes for the first time in your life. There's an opportunity to grieve a loss or feel the relief of a long hoped-for outcome finally come to pass. Traumas that were endured can be released. Confusion that took deep root in your soul can finally be resolved.

Sometimes tears of gratitude emerge at the recognition of a loved one who's there in Spirit World to greet you, or you recognize a beloved friend or family member from a past life, and there's a profound sense of comfort and peace.

When there's a safe space provided for your soul to feel its truth, you can feel immensely healed. Knowing your truth sets your soul free.

Truth can sometimes be lost during the past life that was lived just because it was repressed for valid reasons: such as if you were gay in a place or era where who you were was against the law or punishable by death, or a war interrupted your family, or a sudden death meant you were never able to tell someone how you felt about them.

Your soul thrives with the expression of truth. Blockages to your soul that prevent you from feeling your truth can be cleared in a Past Life Regression.

Yes, that we carry feelings in our souls from life to life is both mysterious and inexplicable. However, tears are so common in regressions that there's no question to me our souls have feelings, memories, and a consciousness beyond a body that knows how to heal.

Who are you and what is your life purpose?

One of my goals is to help you define yourself by your soul and to identify your purpose. As you ask "Who am I?" and "What is my purpose?", you'll discover that whole new universes open up to your imagination and experience.

Since I was a child, these 2 questions have taken me on a lifelong quest.

In my 30's, I was so passionate about this that I devoted myself to finding the answers through spiritual healing. Over the decades of my healing practice, I discovered that when you're open to exploring yourself as divine, there are openings you never imagined which can bring wonderful answers, even life-changing ones.

We carry great burdens from incarnating as humans. Consider the normal way of living on Earth and the fears we face about dying and death and our fear of anything else we don't understand: fear of separation and loss, worry, lack of empowerment, critical self-talk, comparing ourselves negatively with others, living with unbelievable stress that previous generations would find impossible to navigate, and re-cycling many of the same mistakes, still not finding our way out of repeating habits that create great suffering. How can anyone navigate such an impossible realm? Or even begin to find answers?

In Spirit World, your self-perception is enlarged significantly, from a spiritual perspective and infinite landscape. Now, rather than seeing yourself as wrong, guilty, bad, and a failure, you suddenly see yourself with great understanding and you come to know your true self as divine, good, and worthy.

By seeing yourself from a spiritual context, realizations begin to emerge. Generally, it's so freeing that it also relieves you, making space for you to feel more peace and happiness.

A higher perspective

We can all get lost and mired in our troubles. Most of the people coming to me for regressions have things they want to clear, and the beautiful thing about regressions is they work! In a regression you can transcend the state of mind that created the problems.

You need your Spirit Guides and teachers. Spirit World is a place where your guides and teachers come to your aid. We are meant to go to them. It helps when we ask for help, that we are willing to be open and act on the guidance.

You're not meant to do this alone. You're meant to connect with your true self, your Higher Self, your soul! And also to connect with your Spirit Guides and teachers.

You're so much more than your small self. Your soul is infinite because it's divine by nature. Regressions help you to define yourself and your soul purpose.

Your soul is the key factor in all your major life experiences: who you love, what you do, your decisions, your life direction, major crossroads, even your passions and values (which carry across lives).

Unfortunately, your unsolved concerns, tendencies and relationships can also carry over across lifetimes. This is one of the best ways that regressions help, by breaking harmful or confusing patterns holding you back.

You might feel you came here with an important purpose and you strive to stay true to it. But you can get bogged down or distracted by what you see, feel, hear, touch, which can all be very confusing.

Through Spirit World Regression, your life opens up to a whole new dimension. You have crossed the time barrier and transcended the human realm where you are only known by yourself to be human and nothing more. And you discover that, within your soul self, you have answers, and even solutions, and powerful help is available to you from your guides and teachers.

Your soul mate(s)

It's possible, during a Spirit World Regression, for you to discover your primary soul mate. (Sometimes, there is also a secondary soul mate as well.)

These are souls who accompany you during many lifetimes, with whom you share a deep closeness and have agreed to help each other on your soul journeys.

Though they don't always show up as your spouse, sometimes they incarnate in your life as a family member or close friend. These are extraordinary relationships. You and your soul mates make agreements about the role you each can best play in an incarnation.

I feel like the luckiest woman on Earth to be married to my beloved soul mate, Scotty. We absolutely adore each other and have been married for over 27 years, and we've incarnated many, many times together! Doing Spirit World regressions, we continually find each other in our past lives. Scotty has saved my life more than once!

Our marriage has become renewed and immensely deepened from seeing each other's fuller soul identities. It has opened us to greater understanding and compassion for the challenges we encounter in our present lives and has deeply connected us with extraordinary love. Our soul mate love has caused us to treat each other with kindness, honor, and sacredness. When you begin addressing your loved one as a fellow soul, deep respect comes into play.

Chapter 2

Past Life Regression

There are many reasons people arrive at my door for a Past Life Regression.

Most people want to know their life purpose. Many are just curious. Some are grieving. Some are at life crossroads and want to know what direction to take, including questions about whether or not they should move, change jobs, or even stay with their spouse. Some would like to meet their Spirit Guide or to better understand themselves or their hardships.

All these reasons are valid, and you will have your own. I encourage you to trust the experience and information that is given to you during your regression, because it comes from the spiritual realm.

Regression as a source for healing

Past Life Regressions shift something within you, a perception, and your soul can heal through a level of awareness as you release many things held deep within.

Sometimes, with a Past Life Regression, the result can confirm exactly what you were wondering (and had been thinking) was true before you entered your session. It confirms your intuition. With the confirmation will come a larger explanation and probably also guidance and instruction to help you as you go forward.

Other times, there's a resolution to an important life problem, either a new one or an old one.

I'm always so relieved to see the face of my clients when they move from a stressed face to one of great happiness. Although most people don't realize that the healing process also involves transformation, I can tell you that this is what healing is all about.

Transformation can be uncomfortable, but the healing is on the other side. Your commitment to the transformation is where all the gold is.

The beauty of regression is that, in decades of healing work, I've seen it as the most accelerated path to healing.

Sometimes spiritual transformation is hard work, but regression often skips over a lot of discomfort and lets you invoke your healing at the deepest level, the level of your soul.

If you made a list of all the things wrong in your life, you would see your list constitutes where you most suffer. It's a list of your biggest problems, which occupy your time, mind, emotions, and energy. Your list reveals both the story and the source of your most difficult emotional states: discouragement, depression, shame, frustration, anger, aggravation, embarrassment, despair, fear, anxiety, worry, and the list of suffering goes on and on. Many people suffer in silence or "keep a stiff upper lip." This gets lonely.

The items listed are the things that cost your happiness. Listed items also represent areas where you are most stuck. The list has the ability to either hold up your life or, by addressing items on your list, you can enable yourself to be free and move forward.

For the items on your list, the cost is high. They can cost you joy, laughter, ease, well-being, and ability to live a life where you shine, love, have fun, feel meaningful, create, and contribute to others. The question is, "What can you do about your list?"

Some of the things on your list are repeated and can last for many lifetimes. Realizing this, you can face the biggest items on your list, feeling motivated to cross them off in your present life.

For example, there's a Spirit World Regression in this book where the woman had been taught a harsh lesson by a cruel teacher that money interferes with spiritual growth. That past life was over a thousand years ago and the decision she made to favor her spiritual advancement over material wealth of any kind was still operating in her current life creating much suffering.

Another regression revealed a woman who suffered great self-doubt in a past life. It created constant misery for her. I asked her, "How many years have you been stuck with this problem?" She answered, "300 years."

During another regression, it was revealed that my client has been in a contract with her current best friend for over 1500 years. And it was now time to end the relationship, thereby setting her free from experiencing certain enslavements.

By identifying and clearing areas in your current life, you can be free to soar and have a more wonderful life, free of the old stuck energies, which create suffering. Can you see your need for spiritual growth?

Your soul would love for you to step up to the plate and get involved in learning important lessons that you incarnated to learn. That's the whole point of your life.

Consider the things on your list as opportunities to grow. The point of your life is to learn, grow, improve, and to become enlightened until your human self is aligned with your soul and then you are, indeed, a marvel on Earth, a magnificent influence for others as well as yourself. Learning to be guided by your Higher Self leads to your best possible life.

What is a Past Life Regression?

Including your present identity, your soul has been on an eternal journey, learning and growing and incarnating many times to evolve on your path to enlightenment.

The benefits of Past Life Regression are numerous and include:

- Healing
- Receiving spiritual guidance and instruction

- Clarity on where you are in life
- Decreasing your fear of death and dying
- Increasing your intuition
- Meeting your guides
- Recognizing your important relationships and lessons in your present life
- Discovering your life purpose
- Understanding your soul path
- Receiving emotional release and freedom
- Help with whatever you are most struggling with today

What can be addressed in a Past Life Regression?

When you live a life connected to your soul, you live from a place of congruence where more energy, vitality, and intuition are naturally available to you. We all get disconnected sometimes. This is a list of examples of the kinds of things you can successfully address in a past life regression:

- Clear unresolved patterns from a past life into your present life including such things as trauma, a physical problem, a curse, or phobia.
- End unwanted past contracts with people you now realize you are complete with.

- Recognition of people who are in your current life today and for what purpose you know each other now. You can also become aware of what remains to be worked out in your present life with them.

- Dissolve old energy left over from relationships with strong disagreements, or with someone considered an enemy.

- Break a vow which may be blocking your evolution.

- Clear out old cobwebs that might still be affecting your health, prosperity, stress levels, career, emotions, relationships, and your life force energy.

- End fears carried over from lifetime to lifetime which are causing you to feel stuck in your present life since these patterns are repeated, often without knowing why.

- Address recurring health issues which may have roots in a past life where you were wounded or died from something of this same nature or located in the same area of your body.

- Correct the effect of your actions in a past life where you wronged someone. Your guides can help you to clear this.

- Identify your soul - its qualities, patterns, and purpose.

- Let go of things from your past life which you may have carried into your present life such as: past life trauma, sadness, loss, giving up, pride, shame, self-doubt, and similar patterns which cause you suffering and which tend to be repeated from lifetime to lifetime.
- Clarity that you're here for learning, growing, and loving. And this is the purpose of your life rather than to get rich, compete, dominate, or ignore others' needs.
- Identify what brings you real happiness such as: forgiveness (for yourself and others), compassion, lovingkindness, practicing inner peace, accepting responsibilities, seeking wisdom and awareness, and expressing joy.

The study of Past Life Regression brings increased awareness and enlightenment towards living your best life, learning what is most important, and making life choices that align with your soul.

Your Guides

Most people have guides – and they are always with you, whether or not you see or feel them, and they often appear in regressions. For some people, they are their own guide.

Your guides and teachers, in fact, are in charge of the entire session, including the decision to have a regression, as well as choosing a past life, and how to integrate it so that you understand how it applies to your life today.

Being attached to meeting up with one of your Spirit Guides, however, can give the wrong idea that a Past Life Regression isn't of value unless the guide appears. I've found this isn't the case since the regressed state itself originates from the Superconscious, which is your spirituality. It manages your regression with or without a guide. Is it still a spiritual experience? Absolutely!

One of my clients arrived for her regression and during the interview, she revealed that she was in the final stage of cancer. And that, as soon as she left, she was going home to meet with hospice. The reason she came that day to have a regression is that she wanted, and needed, to meet her Spirit Guide.

I saw immediately that the entire success of our session would depend on this one factor, and it gave me concern because, although the majority of people meet their guide, it doesn't happen for everyone, or in the first session.

Fortunately, it worked out that my client's guide showed up right away at the appropriate time during her regression. She had great tears of joy when she met him. She was deeply satisfied and said as she left, she was no longer afraid to die since she felt deeply connected with her guide. She was smiling. So was I!

How you experience a regression is unique

Most everyone has a different way of accessing the information during a regression.

A regression takes place in a different state of mind.

- Some people see their past life as a movie.

- Others see images or have a sense of knowing.
- Some people hear the guidance or hear actual voices.
- Most everyone feels the feelings of the person they were in the past life.

Since we're accustomed to having information confirmed through linear, left-brain logic, you may doubt if the information is accurate. I advise you to trust the information that comes to you. It always works.

Does a regression take place in a trance or hypnotic state?

Yes. Past Life Regression utilizes gentle hypnotherapy. There's an induction period for each of the two kinds of regressions.

Unlike stage hypnosis by performers, Past Life Regression induction is a relaxation technique given by a trained counselor, such as me. The work is approached as sacred, confidential, and highly professional. Its use is for therapy only.

Brainwaves

For the sake of discussing regression, the brainwaves we address are the Beta, Alpha, and Theta.

- B*eta* frequency is the fastest wave. It's your fully awakened state, required when you're talking, reading, doing tasks and such. My goal as a regressionist is to move you out of beta. I do this with simple breathing and relaxing techniques.

- *Alpha* is a slower brain wave like when you meditate, pray, or watch a slow-paced movie late at night. This is the brain wave (at its deeper level) we access for a Past Life Regression. This is pleasantly relaxing and often your voice drops lower with a softer volume.

- *Theta* is the slowest brain wave we access in regressions. This reaches your Super-conscious where your intuition resides. It's useful for the Spirit World Regression, which tends to be longer. This is my favorite brain wave because this is where you discover all the gold nuggets of your soul!

Throughout the session, you can pause, go to the bathroom, cough, or stand up to stretch. You are, at all times, in complete charge and under full control of yourself, though your brain is moving a little slower and you won't feel chatty. It is not advised to use your phone during the brief breaks as this will take you out of the regressed state.

The slower brain waves of Alpha and Theta are necessary for your deep state of relaxation in order to access information from your past lives and Spirit World, to meet your Spirit Guide, and to be able to converse with your Council of Elders.

It's my main job, especially during the first time you have a Past Life Regression, to watch that your level of relaxation remains steady throughout the regression in order for you to access the information about your past lives and Spirit World.

What is the length of time for a Past Life Regression?

The length of a Past Life Regression is about 2 or 2 ½ hours. During a regression, clients often jump time - from current life, past life, to Spirit World and back in a non-linear way.

Preparing for your regression

There are some really important things for you, as a client, to do in order to have a successful regression.

- Stay open and curious throughout.

- Be less concerned with outcomes. Outcomes are often surprising and delightful so you don't need to concern yourself. Allow the regression therapist to guide you. Try not to take control.

- Avoid trying to figure out why you were sent to a particular past life. It will be explained at the end. (This is important because when you use your analytical mind, in order to figure out things - and I realize you are curious! - you leave the regressed trance state, from where all the answers come.)

- There are also two other things that tend to take you out of the regressed state: judging your experience or doubting what is occurring is true. Again, these take you into left brain and are outside the trance state required for a regression. I always ask clients to try and suspend judgment, doubt, and criticism during the entire regression. (I realize that this can be a tall order since you're accustomed to receiving information in a more logical way.) Your curiosity and lack of understanding will be cleared up as you go, and this usually comes toward the end. After your first regression, you won't have doubts that sometimes accompany initial experiences.

What happens during a Past Life Regression?

I often prepare the regression room using Reiki energy to clear the room of negativity for you to have a clean slate.

The session begins with an interview where we chat and share the reason(s) you decided to have a Past Life Regression and what you would like me to know in order for us to work together. There's an exchange of what to expect and any questions you may have. Then we begin.

<u>Set an Intention</u>

Together, we can work through any issue that's on your mind. Setting an intention can mean anything from healing a relationship issue, finances, career stagnation, a big decision facing you - anything that's bothering you that you want to gain insight on and clear.

Clients who book one regression will work with one or more intention. If a client books multiple sessions, more can be worked through over time.

Induction

There's an induction period of about 10 or so minutes where you're taken through a relaxation technique. Scientists have found that the brain can be slowed down to a lower alpha or high theta brain waves state and this is the place to access information from a past life.

Though eyes are closed, while relaxing, you're neither unconscious nor asleep. You're using "active imagination," a term given by Dr. Carl Jung to access the Superconscious.

During the session, if you need to take a break, you can, and then, we resume seamlessly.

Some clients express concern or fear about being regressed, which is totally normal. I've found, in instances where the client has experienced a trauma, especially early childhood trauma, that the regression can be significantly more difficult. And there are many reasons for this, such as the body and psyche are trying to avoid being re-traumatized, or the client may even have Post Traumatic Stress Disorder (PTSD).

Plus, strong defenses have been built around the trauma and breaking through will require taking more time to allow a more gradual trust to be built so that the client can feel safe. I have full respect for this process.

At one point I worked with a client who experienced a lot of childhood trauma and as a young adult she was also violently raped.

We worked for a long time to see if we could get her into an induced state. And, while she finally experienced a past life, it was difficult to keep it going and, unfortunately, it involved a similar trauma in her past life. She kept feeling blocked in the regressed state in spite of wanting to continue. I felt her guides and teachers had, perhaps, selected this particular past life in order to help her clear the trauma. But she just wasn't ready.

If the client can't be regressed within an hour or so, I ask if the client wants to continue. If they're putting up defenses to prevent facing their blocks or fears, it can be tiring so a shorter session making effort towards a successful induction may be required.

In instances like this one, going slowly is paramount to the success of the experience, and honoring your needs is imperative. You may feel like this slow progress is a failure, but as the regression counselor, this protective approach is key. Having more than one regression is the best strategy to gradually overcome the blockage.

If you think you may suffer from PTSD, find a qualified professional to help you. I highly recommend EMDR therapy since these therapists specialize in trauma and work successfully with the U.S. military. I myself have had extensive EMDR and can attest to its value.

Visiting a Past Life

Once induced, when you reach the relaxed state, the session generally opens up to a past life, one which is chosen by your guides and teachers, which they want you to see and for which purpose the guide brought you to the session. Generally, you go from one scene to another, visiting the past life chosen by your guide, until you die in that lifetime, which is quick and painless.

Many people have stated that, as a result of going through a past life regression, they have greatly reduced their fear of death. Some even have no fear of death as a result.

Crossing Over

After the past life death, you find yourself in Spirit World where there's often gentle healing offered following a difficult past life of sadness, hardship, or poverty or from the way you died.

If you get stuck, I explore why. Perhaps it could be from leaving loved ones behind, or fearing Spirit World ahead. We address this entirely in order to clear it.

In regressions, we take the pace of the Superconscious. If it's not moving forward, there's a reason and we'll take time to explore it. Pauses are part of the entire healing experience and it's important to explore further and not skip over any of it.

Spirit Guide(s)

We then try to connect with your guide. As a regressionist, what's most on my mind at this point is to talk with your guide to learn, among other things, how the past life relates to your present life.

Throughout the session I change approaches as needed - sometimes leading you and sometimes following you - as we slowly and tenderly explore the entire experience together. Each regression has its own pace to which I adapt.

I often ask a guide (sometimes there is more than one) for clarification about some of the things that occurred in a past life. Sometimes you may have more than one past life and we explore each to make sure we understand what purpose each of them served and how each one relates to your current life.

I also take notes so I can keep track of each life and each scene as well as important guidance given from Spirit World. On the notes, I draw a star next to things I want to return to that need more clarification and also to be able to repeat the sequence to you after the regression has ended.

It helps to have feedback from an informed listener in the role of regressionist in a safe and nurturing environment.

Exit Interview

At the end of the session, there's an exit interview where you share what you thought about your experience and begin to integrate it. I also share my insights and healing intuition during this period to help you see your life in a higher context.

As a regression therapist, I'm in a position of following you and hearing your own personal impressions and interpretations, as you are the one most likely to know the applications. I often find myself repeating something that happened during your past life and then saying, "What did you think of that?" And, if I have an intuition, I may reflect it back and add, "Does this sound about right to you?"

Throughout the regression, I'm highly engaged, like an explorer who is sleuthing to discover the treasures of the soul. My job is to help bring to light as much information as possible, which can be attained in no other way. I bring my highest gifts to you as a healer, including a great deal of understanding, care, spiritual oversight, and compassion for your brave journey.

Chapter 3

Spirit World Regression

The next level of Past Life Regression

I feel that Spirit World Regressions are where the greatest resources for your life and healing can be discovered.

Spirit World is accessed through your Superconscious, which holds all the records of who you are and what your purpose is throughout all your lifetimes. It's the location of your soul between lives.

Spending time in Spirit World during regression is the most sacred of experiences where you gain insight and receive guidance from your Spirit Guide and your spiritual teachers, such as the Council of Elders, White Light, or other angelic entities.

I find that as a regression counselor, healer, and individual who loves to go deep, this work is intriguing, awakening, healing, and deeply meaningful. There's so much valuable, eye-opening information available to you about yourself. For these reasons it's become the culmination of my life's work.

Spirit World Regressions are different from Past Life Regressions in many ways.

We always start a Spirit World Regression with a visit to a past life. Then, once through a few scenes, you cross over into Spirit World.

Once in Spirit World, you can gain benefits and information such as:

- Your identity as a soul and your unique soul characteristics.
- Your life purpose.
- Meeting and interacting with your Spirit Guide(s).
- Connecting with your primary source for divine guidance (e.g. an archangel, Mother Mary, a spiritual teacher, an indistinct but trusted spiritual source, a Great Light, or your Council of Elders).
- The identity of your primary soul mate and sometimes a secondary soul mate.
- Discovery of your Soul Family, identifying people in your current life as those who repeat many lives together with you, as well as spiritually focused work you do with your Soul Family in Spirit World. You may be in a study group working with others on common goals for your lives on Earth.
- Discovering if you're an Earth-based soul or if you come from another galaxy or planet, or a place without density. Or if you're from the Angelic Realm, or straight from Source.
- The percent of energy you brought with you into this current life and if it's enough. Most

souls bring about 60-80% of their energy for incarnations, according to what you will need. We leave the remaining energy in Spirit World, where we do important spiritual work. Highly experienced souls often bring less energy to Earth.

- If you are currently having a split or parallel life.

But even more importantly, you can establish a relationship with Spirit World and your guides and teachers and thereby gain a strong sense of never again feeling alone. You have guidance!

You can connect with them all you want! And you can learn how to access them anytime. Learning to live by a daily check-in with your inner guides can change your life for the better.

This takes dedication. And multiple Spirit World Regressions help you to gain more information about yourself and establish the life you want, aligned with your Higher Self and its purpose, for a powerful life.

You'll want to explore for what reason the guides and teachers selected the particular past life shown, and to understand how it relates to your present life.

Many people have stated that, as a result of going through a Past Life Regression they reduce their fear of death. This is especially true for Spirit World Regressions because you spend most of the regression in Spirit World and it quickly becomes evident that you surpassed death as you explore the expanded world of your soul.

What is the brain wave state in a Spirit World regression?

For the deeper and longer regression of a Spirit World Regression, you'll need to be in Theta brain wave, the very relaxed state. In this state, you're able to access the Superconscious mind where your biggest gems of information about yourself are found.

The two biggest words I hear used to describe these regressions are, "Amazing!" and "Fascinating!"

In the regressed state, there can be big insights, revelations, realizations, and much enlightenment about your life and your soul. I began regression work because I wanted to explore and make endless discoveries about my soul. And it can be mind-blowing as well as healing.

I find that your Spirit Guide will usually choose the path of clearing you from something first before introducing you to yourself as a soul. The clearing can be life changing.

What to Expect in a Spirit World Regression

The length of a Past Life Regression is about 2 hours, whereas the length of a Spirit World Regression is about 3 ½ hours. There are many similarities but the difference between these types of regressions is astounding.

The length of the induction is significant in that it's longer in order to enable you to drop deeply enough into the regressed state to access and sustain Spirit World for that length of time.

The main benefits of a Spirit World Regression (versus a Past Life Regression), are gained from spending more time in Spirit World with your guides and teachers, where your learning and awakening ascend with power like a rocket boost to give you a 140,000 mile high view of yourself.

During this period, you'll receive insights, healing, and guidance on your life and purpose. Specific instructions are often provided. Their goal is to help you to fulfill your soul's purpose for your present life and also to take a look back on what you've been learning from past lives and how this is connected to your current life. During this process your mind will be opened to vast understanding of yourself.

Interview

The interview begins the same way as a Past Life Regression. I spend about 30 minutes with you to determine the primary reason you came and what things are most important for you to learn or address in our time together.

In a Spirit World regressed state - because the induction trance is deeper - you won't be able to keep track of the vast amount of information received, though you can recall as I review the regression with you at the end or while listening to the recording later.

For the Spirit World Regression, I ask you to bring a list of the top 10 people with whom you've had a personal relationship and have been closest to or who've had the greatest significance in your entire life. The reason I ask for the top 10 list of people is that often, one or more of them may appear in the regression.

In addition, I ask that you bring 4-6 questions for your guides and teachers. During the interview, we review the top 10 people along with questions for your guides, to be sure I have understanding. Since I just met you, these are ways that help keep me in the loop of information as it unfolds to you and for me to be most helpful to you as your regression counselor. Based on your questions, we may set an intention for the regression.

Induction

Though your eyes are closed, while relaxing, you're neither unconscious nor asleep. Dr. Carl Jung coined the term: *active imagination*.

He found that this Superconscious self-accessed information from your soul is primal and reliable. In my experience, the Superconscious offers a startling overview of your life and even your past lives. Learning the context of your many lives and what you've been working to accomplish immediately increases your understanding to see yourself more clearly.

In the deeper regressed state of the Spirit World Regression, your brain operates at a much slower pace. This Theta brain wave is the ideal state to access the deeper, Superconscious information.

Past Life

The Past Life Regression session opens to a past life, one which is chosen by your guides and teachers, which they want you to see.

We go from one scene to another, visiting the chosen past life or lives, until you have a brief death scene from the last past life shown. I find that even if you die violently from an accident, an attack, or by murder, it's not felt or experienced as real by you today, as you relax in my recliner. And, I make sure we don't dwell on the dying process but keep moving on to crossing over.

Spirit World

The Newton Institute refers to the different places you can be taken to in between lives - in Spirit World - as stations. Here are the most common ones I have repeatedly encountered in Spirit world:

Cleansing/Restoration

A purifying or cleansing generally takes place once you arrive in Spirit World. There may be lights or beings subtly working on you to help clear your energies from your past life. You become aware that something pleasant is occurring to you – perhaps a soothing or tingling sensation which, afterwards, relives you of past life negative energies, leaving you feeling refreshed. After this, you're ready to continue your journey in Spirit World.

This is where you go after death. It's considered home for yourself and your Soul Family. Visiting Spirit World in a regression is a positive experience. Your guides and teachers cause you to feel loved and they're compassionate towards your journey to other realms in order to help you learn all that you can.

Spirit Guide

Usually you're greeted, after your cleanse, by your Spirit Guide who spends some time with you as you acclimate to its presence. Sometimes there are tears when meeting your Spirit Guide. I then pause so you can take in these amazing energies.

I always ask for your guide to appear. And, most often, but not always, your Spirit Guide appears to you.

Some people have multiple guides and your guides may change according to your growth and what your specific needs are for your present level of development.

Your guide may appear as an impressive bright White Light or a Golden Light or a male or female being or even a green-eyed cat!

Sometimes guides choose not to show themselves. I believe, when this happens, they're creating a demand for you to flex your spiritual muscle and reach for them. It strengthens and expands your intuitive ability and your trust in it.

Council of Elders

The Council of Elders are the ones who select the past life you visit during a regression. They usually appear in a Spirit World Regression, where deeper answers are revealed, and not in a Past Life Regression.

They explain why they chose the particular past life and how the past life applies to your life today. You immediately connect with everything they're explaining to you about the deepest things about yourself. It's an eye-opening, often mind-blowing, psychic experience.

Meeting with your Council is one of the most auspicious, powerful, and sacred of all experiences in Spirit World.

There's generally a feeling of awe and deep respect when you meet with them. They treat you with loving regard as a sacred being.

They meet with you to help clarify your life. You can ask them questions and interact with them. (e.g. What's my life purpose? Why am I having such a hard time?)

The Elders:

- Are highly evolved beings, full of love and wisdom for you. They're charged with overseeing all of your lives and your evolution as a soul.
- Bring enormous clarity to who you are and your life purpose.
- Are available to help you to understand yourself.
- Are focused on your soul's spiritual welfare and its ability to grow & evolve, which involves learning important spiritual lessons that can only be learned from living out your lives. The more you grow, the more wisdom you acquire.
- You can call on them anytime for guidance and help. They're your spiritual team.

In general, there's a Council spokesperson who addresses you. Other elders may also engage in dialogue with you.

Most people visit a Council of Elders during a Spirit World Regression. However, sometimes, the guides and teachers will choose for you to access their information through your Superconscious. It works just as well.

The Council is where you and I ask the important questions that you brought for your Spirit World Regression.

Every Spirit World Regression is different from others and often very surprising. Even before I have an opportunity to ask your questions brought to the regression, the Council may address your questions They may choose to address your questions through your Superconscious, where you access your clair-cognizance of "knowing."

Your Council and guide are the ones who brought you to the regression, and who selected us to be together, and they already know which past life to select and the reason for selecting it as well as how it relates to what is currently going on in your life or most concerns you. They're fully in charge of your entire regression experience.

Garden

Once you're in Spirit World, you may find yourself in a beautiful garden.

It's an inspiring and uplifting place to rest and enjoy yourself on your Spirit World journey. Sometimes, important meetings take place in the Garden with your guide(s). Sometimes people who were once close to you, who passed on, may appear to you and cause you to feel their love.

The Library or Temple of Knowledge

This is a place where you go to select your body and to design your next life, including the one you are presently in. You have a great deal of assistance from your guides and teachers on these important decisions.

You can also review past lives from the pages in the living books. When you open each page, the images come alive and you can watch the scene.

Source

Some souls return directly to Source or to a state of Consciousness of "All That Exists." I don't consider this a station. It's more like a home for your soul.

From there, you experience a primal state of pure awareness where you feel utterly complete and you want for nothing. Because of its omni-power, it's almost impossible to describe.

Questions for your guide

Once you meet your Spirit Guide, I pause for a moment to see if the guide starts with guidance or explanation of the past life shown to you. I like the guide to take the lead. However, sometimes they're waiting for my lead to come in with your list of questions.

I go through your list of questions, one at a time, checking in with you to see if the guide's answer made sense to you and if it was sufficiently addressed for you.

We may need more clarification. Sometimes, what the guide says may bring up more things to ask about. Generally, the guides give us plenty of time to cover everything. This is the point of a Spirit World Regression. We have the time for in-depth questioning and to gain deeper understanding.

You may want to know about your future. Questions about your future may or may not receive an answer.

First of all, the guides are more focused on helping you with your present life. They bring you into a past life (or multiple ones) in order to most help you with what you need now.

There's another reason they generally don't answer questions about your future (even though I may ask these questions anyway on your behalf.) At all times, your free will influences multiple possibilities and outcomes in your present life. Your guides and teachers will not interfere with free will as this is part of your human experience. But they do have a way of conveying all that you need to know during a particular regression.

Some Spirit World Regressions are shorter than others. And some go the full extent of the time allotted. Your guides know how much time you have and they're geniuses at conveying exactly what is appropriate for you.

Multiple regressions are required for a fuller understanding of your soul. But even in one Spirit World Regression, you can gain an extraordinary amount that will be enormously helpful to your present life. The guidance is incredibly powerful and valuable. You have an immense support system on Earth through your guides.

So far, a Spirit World Regression sounds fairly simple, that is, until you find yourself riding in a spaceship to target certain planets to heal by using color or you become engulfed in a magnificently all powerful White Light, or you discover you're part of a collective who has incarnated to help save the planet, or you see yourself as a magnificent master whose light body is 27,000 miles long.

Anything can happen in a regression! Some are more bizarre than others but even the lower-keyed regressions are equally powerful to help you understand yourself and your present life.

I find that if you're in an important or pivotal moment in your present incarnation, your guides and teachers often focus on just that. Overall, people generally find enormous help from the guidance received and this tends to be the main reason clients return for more regressions. There's much information to explore, in fact, it's endless. All of the information is empowering and intriguing and frequently life changing.

The Review

Throughout the session I lead you step by step and take notes so I can put all the information together at the end of the regression for your review which helps integrate the enormous amount of information received while in the regressed state.

Generally, because of the longer length of time, the amount of information received, and the depth of a Spirit World Regression, I recommend that you take quiet time afterwards to reflect on and journal your experience. (Actually, I recommend that for any type of regression.)

There's often a wow factor to the Spirit World experience and generally, there's more to process than the Past Life Regression. There are often wonderful and unimaginable surprises to discover!

At the end of your Spirit World Regression, you share what you thought about your regression experience.

This helps to begin integrating it. I also share my insights and healing intuition to help you see your life in the context of your soul. During the review, we try to recapture the treasures gained from the experience and apply it to your present life. Understanding how the regression applies to your present life is critical to the success of the regression. There's plenty of information to process!

An important part of any regression for me as a regression counselor and healer is to add intuitive insights that may help you to identify your individual soul, based on your Spirit World Regression experience. This is important information to gain. I make notes during your regression based on what I see or sense, for sharing later. Sometimes, my intuition matches with the experience as it unfolds so it may not be necessary.

Spirit World healing

I've seen many regressions which were life changing. The effects have been lasting and profound with healing. There's no greater, faster, easier way to bring healing than through Spirit World Regressions.

You discover that you are a soul! And that you have a purpose!

Your soul yearns to be seen and to receive understanding from you. I've found no more powerful way to have answers to your life's questions than to dive into multiple regressions where a world of truth awaits you. It helps you to begin unraveling the very long journey you've been on as a soul, going from lifetime to lifetime, learning and growing. You'll discover some of the things you've gone through in order to learn your biggest lessons and become who you are today – a soul on a journey of immense learning!

PART 2

Past Life Regression Stories

Chapter 4

Clearing Blocks of Sadness and Depression

Vicki greeted me with smiling, beautiful brown eyes. She was in her early 20's, just graduated with her master's degree, and was curious to know about her past lives.

Her intention was to find out about any soul contracts, karma, and the lessons she's supposed to be learning.

Past life daughter

Her past life opened where she was standing in a field with trees. She wore a red dress and black shoes. Vicki felt peaceful.

The next scene, Vicki was in her kitchen watching her 4-year-old daughter play. She wore a deep purple colored dress. (I sensed the color would be important.)

Vicki was feeling happy and in awe of her pretty little girl! As feelings of love and appreciation were building, the two embraced, feeling deep affection for each other. Vicki commented, "It's a lot of love!" Vicki was beaming by the discovery of their immense love.

Then, Vicki found herself, once again, in a field, alone. She was feeling sad because her husband had left her. In response to her sadness, Vicki decided to "let him go." (I thought of the great resilience of her soul!)

In another scene, she and her daughter were in an outdoor market buying food. They were holding hands as they shopped. The daughter went to a table wanting to buy something, but Vicki said she didn't have enough money for it. She felt guilty as the little girl pulled at her arm, wanting the item.

We went directly to Vicki's last day. She was a young 30-year-old with a life-threatening condition. Sitting on the side of the bed at night, she felt deeply sad from being left alone without a partner. She quickly passed on. I believe that she died because she was so broken with hopelessness and depression from her loneliness and poverty.

Spirit World

As she crossed over to Spirit World, I asked if she felt she needed to energetically say goodbye to her daughter. She did not.

Looking over her life, she felt it had been a sad life without enough money and being unpartnered. However, the highlight and lovely surprise had been her daughter, who had meant a great deal to her.

Once in Spirit World, Vicki was greeted by a large presence (house-sized) which made her feel calm. It helped to clear the energy of sadness from her past life.

When we called upon her Spirit Guide, Vicki became aware of a deep purple colored form of energy that appeared. Vicki confirmed that this was her Spirit Guide. I asked if we could ask some questions and her Spirit Guide indicated yes.

I asked, "For what purpose was Vicki shown this particular past life?"

The Guide said it was about the little girl. "You haven't met her yet. She'll come into your present life as your daughter. Be patient."

Vicki was excited to learn this news because she and the daughter in that life had shared such deep love and affection for each other.

I asked, "For what purpose will you reunite with her?"

Her Spirit Guide answered that Vicki will be learning something from her. And the little girl will be coming to learn from her as well. This will be a second chance for Vicki. The last time had been sad because of her husband's departure and impoverishment. This life will be more fun for them.

I asked if this was Vicki's karma. The Guide answered, "Yes, because Vicki had left the daughter behind when she died early and, yet, Vicki had an obligation to her. Now her soul can clear the slate."

I asked if this would happen within the next 5-10 years. The guide answered yes.

I asked the guide to please share what Vicki's present life purpose is.

The answer was twofold:

First, Vicki needed to pay back her debt to the child for having to abandon her through her early death.

Second, Vicki needed to stop suffering from guilt. I asked Vicki if this made sense to her and she said it did. She explained that when she left to move to San Diego, she also left behind an important relationship.

And although it was the best thing for her to do, she felt guilty for leaving.

I asked the Spirit Guide purple energy if guilt was a theme in more than one of Vicki's past lives. The answer was yes.

The guide told me "It's okay. I will help her."

I was having a hard time reading Vicki's emotions, so I asked her in a more positive way to please rate the amount of comfort on a scale between 1-10 she was receiving now from this regression. Vicki stated a 7. (When emotions are not transparent, I often use the scale between 1 and 10 to help me understand at what level something is being felt.)

I asked how much inner self comfort she brought to our session. She answered a 3. This was helpful because I had no idea she was so low on comfort, as she wasn't a person who showed or shared her feelings. Because of the regression, Vicki's level of comfort had risen from a 3 to a 7. That's progress!

We learned that there was another reason for which she was brought to the regression. It was about her joy, or lack of it. Vicki told me she had someone special in her life who had rejected her, and it hurt her deeply. She carried a lot of sadness from this. And she still longed to be in a relationship with this person.

I asked the purple energy to please help her.

Vicki was handed an orange colored ball. Holding it in her hand, she felt great warmth. I asked how warm it was. She said it was so warm that it was almost hot. She received an energy from it and it had the effect of lifting her joy and hope.

She described it as "powerful and creative and exciting." Until this point in the regression, Vicki had barely shown any emotion, so expressing positiveness was a new expression for her.

I asked, "What effect does this ball of energy have on your joy?"

Vicki said, "The energy reclaims my joy." I asked, "On a scale between 1-10, to what extent is the orange energy effectively helping you?" She felt it was effective at an 8.

I asked her to rate her level of joy before the orange ball energy. Vicki said it was at a 5. And, she sensed that her level of joy would increase as she went forward so there wouldn't be further suffering.

I commented that now that Vicki knows she has a powerful Spirit Guide, she can come to him anytime and for the rest of her life. Vicki acknowledged this and agreed.

I was surprised to learn during our exit interview that Vicki never wanted a family. But now she wanted a family and was eager and excited to be reunited with the little girl again as her daughter! This was a life changer!

This is what I observed:

- Vicki was a quiet, soft spoken woman who was not talkative throughout the regression. At the end of our session, I asked her, "Are you usually this quiet?" And, "Does this mean that you tend to process things deeply without having things you're thinking about come to the surface?" She answered in the affirmative.

I speculate this meant that there were many nuances that were omitted from my clear understanding of the regression. However, even without more detail, I felt we had a very clear session.

- I was curious that Vicki was wearing a deep purple colored dress in the happy kitchen scene with her daughter when they hugged and exchanged love for each other. It felt like a synchronistic moment, because later in the session, when she met her guide, her guide was also deep purple colored. I felt as though her Spirit Guide subtly made a point of revealing its presence as the purple color at the happy kitchen scene. I also sensed that its guiding presence was what brought forth the intense moment of great love and affection, which accented a bright light in her life with her daughter. Look for these clues. Guides do that!

- I was surprised that Vicki felt comfort from her guide at only a 7 and not a 9 or 10. And I had no idea that when she arrived, her level of comfort was about a 3 as there had been no indication of this. I realized how deeply and stoically she carried her emotions and her information. I was also relieved to know that her Spirit Guide was offering her a great deal of clearing as well as healing of her sadness and guilt, and her guide had brought her to our session for those very reasons.

- Because of the sadness from being alone during her past life, and also her suffering from guilt, I hoped Vicki would open up more so that we could address these pains from a larger perspective. However, I walk a fine line as a healer not wanting to pry or intrude on someone's privacy or their choice not to disclose. Out of great respect for her soul and boundaries, I let go of the need to help reveal and heal everything at deeper levels.

- Of all my Past Life Regressions, only one other time has a client expressed the intentions that Vicki did: to understand her soul contracts, her karma, and what she's supposed to be learning. And, as it turned out, these were very specific to exactly what her Spirit Guide revealed and the purpose for which she wanted a past life regression. These were the reasons for which her guide brought her to the regression. She gained the knowledge and exciting news that her life will include the role of being a mother and that she had a Spirit Guide to turn to for further healing of guilt and sadness. These were very uplifting discoveries! Vicki also gained the knowledge that, as she had sensed, she had karma to complete with her daughter, and it was a soul contract. This gave Vicki a new perspective from which to look at her present life and its meaningful contracts and karma. This is exactly what she was hoping to discover.

- Unlike her past life when she lived in poverty, in her current life she had the financial means to take care of herself and her daughter. They each had important things to learn from each other which would enable them to complete their past karma together.

Chapter 5

Healing Childhood Trauma and Reuniting with God's Presence

When I met Henry, within moments of him walking in I felt his deep, beautiful love. A man in his mid-50's, he emanated a gentle, masculine strength as well as a warm smile.

When we sat down for his interview, he informed me that his life was in transition, as he had just ended a business with a partner. Now he was ready to move forward. Henry had decided to move to Spain, where his ancestry was from, and where he planned to farm. He called it his "final move."

However, as he talked about why he had come for a regression, Henry described a great emotional pain he carried in the pit of his stomach which came from a traumatic incident that occurred in his childhood.

And he's carried this pain for his entire life. Without giving me details, he referred to rough neighborhood boys who did something to him which caused him great disturbance and fear.

As a boy, he was confused by it and couldn't understand it. As a man, he's carried it as a block and it has caused him to be blocked from intimacy in his relationships, including with his wife.

Henry was shown several past lives, which gave clues about his soul's character and his long journey to find peace.

A soldier in Germany saying farewell to his family

In the first past life, the scene opened with him in freezing cold temperatures during World War II in Germany winter. Henry was in his 40's. He and another decorated soldier were stranded outside standing by a meager fire, which was useless to warm them.

Continuing with the story, it was too late. They had been left and the enemy was rapidly approaching. He felt scared.

In his dying moment, his thoughts and love went to his wife, mother, and brother back home. He tenderly spoke of how much he loved them and would miss them. I felt his deep connection and love for them, which was part of the character of his loving soul. He was passionate about love and family.

In additional past lives, a theme of love emerged as Henry was shown women partners who he loved with a special, soulful love. Here are a few of those examples.

Soul mate past life

In one past life, Henry met his soul mate, Antoinette.

As soon as they met, he discovered that "she was the love of his life." He wore a huge smile from the moment that he met her and his smile grew bigger throughout our conversation.

I asked how he felt when he was with her. He told me that he "felt and loved her soul." I felt his love showed a depth of spirituality. He told me tearfully that ever since they had to part, early on, that as he went on with that life, he hurt every single day. And he always felt her with him. I noted how passionately he loved her.

Stone mason on Malta

In another past life, Henry was a head mason in charge of building a great wall on Malta Island.

At the moment of completion, he spontaneously looked up and saw a girl at the end of his wall. Seeing her, he opened his heart and broke into a huge smile. Her name was Maria, but he recognized her as Antoinette, his soul mate from the previous past life. Telling me about her, he lit up, thrilled to see her. She had come into his life to be with him once again. However, we were to quickly learn, as before, that they had to separate.

Together before

In another past life, Henry had a wife named Melinda and a young son. I asked if his wife was his soul mate Antoinette. He said it was not. It was a different woman. And he then showed great passion saying that he loved and adored her.

As we continued the regression, he suddenly realized that she was actually his current wife! And that in this present life, they reincarnated to be together once again. And, now, they were going to repeat living a life in Spain on a farm, just like before!

African Jew

In his final past life, he was an African Jew with his wife, Laleen. He described her as "a great soul". He felt deeply connected and had nothing but unconditional love for her. The theme is, again, all about unconditional love and a soul connection with a woman.

Now I had seen his profound love in several of his past lives. He showed great joy about each woman's soul and how his love was attracted to their soul. It was the description of something pure and spiritual. Clearly, he appreciated a love that was pure, whether it was with family members or children but especially with his extraordinary women, yet he was a man who had also experienced heartbreaking losses of being separated from all the people he had loved.

We had been shown many separations from loved ones in these past lives. I wondered, how does someone learn to adapt to so many losses through past lives?

Henry entered Spirit World

Now everything was about to shift. Henry died at the end of the final past life as an African Jew. Crossing over to Spirit World, Henry found himself sitting in a very well-lit space. The light was warm and white. It calmed him.

Next, Henry felt a presence, which presented itself as an older man. His name was Ray and he was Henry's Spirit Guide.

We asked, "For what purpose was Henry shown these particular past lives?"

The answer came immediately. The "force of love" led Henry's lives. It was explained that in order to progress, however, he would always have to let go of something. This meant he would have to be strong.

I asked, "What were the things you were learning to let go of?" He said that one of the things he had to learn to let go was fear of losing his loved ones.

Henry then became very serious as he changed the subject. He reminded me that he currently lives with a lot of fear which he carries in the pit of his stomach. He went on to say that he puts up a wall for self-protection, even from his wife, shutting her out. He was blocked and said that he was stuck in fear and had no peace whatsoever.

We had been shown that Henry's soul was naturally and passionately full of pure love. And, I felt that his childhood traumas had interrupted his soul's natural flow of trusting in love and the feeling of being safe to love.

Henry also shared that when he entered his present life, it was only with 50% peace. He said that he was shown that when he was the African Jew, over 400 years ago in his last life, as he was dying, he felt God's great love and adoration for him.

It was a stand-out moment and it gave him immense inner peace. It was the first time he'd ever felt this and he hadn't had that kind of peace since then. This God Presence had been missing in his life for 400 years until today. And it's the one thing his soul most longed for and needed.

I was finding myself gaining more understanding about his soul and that, although he had loved others in a pure and spiritual way, and even dealt with grief when he lost his loved ones, Henry carried a very old, unresolved fear.

The regression deepened to reveal that his soul seemed to be longing for God.

I felt a healing message come through for him: We had been shown during our session that Love was one of the major themes of his past lives, and it revealed Henry's Higher Self. Seeing evidence from his past lives, I could see how divine Love guided his soul and he allowed it to do so.

I was led to speak to Henry as a guide. I explained that divine Love was more powerful than anything - including the griefs from his past lives and the traumas of his childhood and its memories and lingering feelings.

Love had been guiding his past lives, just as it was today. He was totally receptive to this healing message. Henry was in tune with Love's power and it all made sense to him. He told me, a little tearfully, that he had now returned to feeling close to God. It meant the world to him!

After I completed the healing message, he said he was feeling much stronger. Something – a dark shadow – was lifted off him. He said that he no longer felt anxious or blocked, even in the pit of his stomach, which he had lived with since childhood. It had all left him.

Then, I asked to rate his peace on a scale from 1-10. He smiled and said it was a 10. Henry left with a heart filled with gratitude and a big hug of thanks.

This is what I observed:

- During the regression, Henry shared with me the strength he gained from the struggle of having blamed himself for the trauma in his childhood. He had to face it. He explained that he felt it was imperative to gain this strength in order to move forward in his life.

- Recalling his dying experience 400 years ago as an African Jew in his last life, when he felt God's presence profoundly with him, he felt reunited with this divine presence. And it also helped him to connect with this divine presence when he realized the pure love he carried in his past lives. This presence would give him the peace he so longed for and deserved, a peace that he'd not experienced in 400 years.

- Later, I researched the defense wall of Malta. It was described as the most powerful artificial fortress in the world, originally built around the Bronze Age settlements. I discovered that the wall was built over thousands of years. Henry had a big hand in this project.

- During our lives on Earth, one of the things we have the hardest time with is when we become separated from a loved one. Henry was shown countless dear loved ones from his past lives and he was shown his separation from them all. As a result, he learned how to face loss, let it go, and the importance of moving forward.

- As a result of the regression, Henry was, once again, able to move forward. This time it was towards the divine, which had been unexpressed within his soul for many centuries. His reuniting with God meant the world to him and even released him from dark shadows and emotional wounds that had accompanied him most of his life.

Chapter 6

Lean on Your Guides and Know You Are Not Alone

A quiet, polite Indian man presented himself at the door. Rajan spoke excellent English with his endearing Indian accent.

During the interview, I learned that he'd come to the U.S. alone, to study software electrical engineering, about 15 years ago. I would guess he was in his late 30's.

He had typed about 9 or 10 questions for his guide. I shared that we would do our best to have as many of these answered as possible.

However, given the complexities of his questions, I told him it might require a deeper and longer regression (a Spirit World Regression) to address everything.

His list included questions like, "Is my suffering over now?" And, "What am I supposed to learn in this life? What is my purpose?" And, "How is my father? (who passed on) And, "Does he have a message for me?" Also, "Is there any advice on how I can spend the rest of my life with confidence and happiness?" And, "Why do bad things always happen when I eat meat?"

I loved his curiosity! It took a while to get him regressed but I persisted.

There were 2 brief past lives presented. They each came to an abrupt stop. This is not unusual. Your guide deliberately reveals only what is pertinent for you at the time.

A castaway

The first past life opened where he was a castaway in an old fishing ship. It was the 1800's and he was desperate to go home. He had lost everything, his clothes tattered, his beard long and unkempt. It sounded as though he was barely surviving. There was no further information. He was taken immediately to another past life.

Murdered

The second past life opened with Rajan alone, late at night, taking a walk in a dangerous part of town. A man appeared who had a wild look about him. Rajan immediately knew he was in danger.

Then suddenly the bearded man chased him until Rajan fell and the man was on top of him with a large knife. Rajan was trapped underneath him. He was stabbed in the neck. As he described this, Rajan touched his neck indicating the exact place being stabbed. The man who stabbed him was dressed in rags like a homeless person. There was a lot of blood. Rajan died from the stabbing.

By quickly completing 2 past lives and then crossing over, it meant that we could spend the majority of our time in Spirit World where his questions could be explored as well as the identification of his soul. Just what he had hoped!

For the next hour, Rajan often expressed doubt about everything happening. He said it felt as though he were making it all up. This is common for a client's first time being regressed.

If you have a job like Rajan who worked as an engineer, a job that depends on being able to verify what is reliable and logical, it can be more challenging to trust your psyche through the process of regression, which is not linear.

Rajan expressed during our interview that he did not often listen to his intuition. This would not, however, prevent him from having a successful Past Life Regression.

The Superconscious is where all our memory is stored and for all time. Resourcing it is a spiritual adventurer's dream come true! I was surprised, that from someone who's not attuned to his intuition how quickly he came to Spirit World. He had managed to bypass his doubts - without any blocks - to successfully cross over.

His Spirit Guides

In Spirit World, Rajan was immediately met by a being who wore all white and had large white wings. The wings were folded, not spread. We would come to discover that this was his Spirit Guide who was accompanied by another secondary guide. In addition, there were 2 less prominent guides. There were 4 in all.

His main guide's name was Guildo and his secondary guide's name was Brian. They wanted to take him somewhere.

Rajan next described a scene that had a huge sky and bright, shining, sunny light. It was the entire universe! There was no one around. They headed towards the bright, shining light and traveled as fast as a spaceship, watching all the stars zoom by rapidly.

Healing and Restoration in Spirit World

Then, the ship stopped, and they arrived, still in the light. Things had calmed a lot. The sky was dark, and he could see stars. As he walked on the huge, beautiful universe, he was surrounded by twinkling stars.

There were millions of these tiny stars and they began showering him like healing projections of light. He was passing through them as they began showering him from head to toe. The shower caused a tingling sensation all over his face and hands. He said that it felt good and was helpful.

I knew that this was a much-needed period of healing and restoration given to souls who have had a difficult life, especially with the trauma of his murder.

I allowed the healing period to go as long as was necessary. When it ended, I asked if he felt that the fear and trauma had come over into his current life, or did he feel it was now behind him? He stated that he felt this was completely healed.

Regressions can be immensely helpful for clearing things that you brought from past lives, including traumas, phobias, and blocks that can create suffering and hold you back in your present life. I felt relieved that the direness of his 2 past lives had not carried over.

Then his Spirit Guide Guildo said, "Let's go!" They took him to a place where Brian then told him, "Relax here and have a drink."

He was still in Spirit World's outer space. As he sat and relaxed, peaceful showers of White Light appeared once again and this time they were streaming from his feet towards his head. His job was to relax. Apparently, the guides felt he needed additional healing to restore his energy and spiritual essence.

Now they were once again on the move. I asked where they were heading. Rajan informed me that Guildo and Brian had their hands around his shoulders as they traveled, and their hands felt good to him. He added that their touch was contributing to his confidence so that he knew that he was not alone. (I learned that he needed this message).

They went through a huge dark tunnel. When they came out of the tunnel he was at a table with 5 chairs facing him. The atmosphere was very friendly.

The Council of Elders

Rajan was instructed to sit on the other side of the table and his guides sat with him.

There were beings sitting across from him. This was his Council of Elders where he could gain important information about how he was progressing in his current life, as well as receive helpful instruction. (The Council of Elders is one of the stations that mostly occurs in a Spirit World Regression and not typically a Past Life Regression.)

The being in the middle, sitting across from him was the spokesperson. We asked him, "For what reason did you show Rajan the past life as a stowaway on a shipping vessel?"

This question was followed by a large download of the story that would explain.

As a stowaway, Rajan had gone through all his money and was trying to save his life and go back home for help. He was desperate but he made it.

And his parents and brother and sister greeted him when he arrived after being a stowaway. He indicated that his difficult experience on the ship had been painful. His life had hit rock bottom.

Rajan swore he would never make that mistake again. "What mistake?" I asked. He explained that he had run away from home searching for his fortune in gold. It had gone horribly.

We learned that he made a blind decision and took a huge risk. This created a desperate condition, threatening his very survival.

Rajan wanted to make it big in that past life. But the mistake he made was that he took action without consideration or a plan. He suffered from impetuosity. And this wouldn't be the last time.

Rajan went on to share that this is why the Council had shown him these 2 past lives. More information would come as we met with them. The Council continued their telepathic communication with Rajan.

In the second past life, he was a well-dressed man who had taken a risk at night walking alone in an area that wasn't safe. He impetuously made the decision to go to the dangerous area for a late-night walk without weighing the risk.

The Council said, "Be smart. Don't dig for gold or try to win the lottery. Don't take the shortcut by avoiding the need to earn your way. What you think may be quick and easy is loaded with risk."

I asked if he had learned this lesson or did he also suffer from this in his present life?

He answered that he still suffered from impetuosity though he felt that he was doing much better in this life.

In his past lives he lost everything.

However, in this current life, he made the right decision when he decided to move to the United States from India. It was not a risk.

This idea had come to him intuitively and he decided to follow it.

We asked the Council how he was doing in his present life. They told Rajan that he was receiving a lot of help from his guides and others and that's why he survived the stowaway past life. We asked the Council for instruction to help him do even better.

They generously gave it. The Council said that Rajan needed to become quieter and calmer, to listen to his thoughts, begin meditating and continue with his practice of prayer. Most of all, Rajan needs to start tuning into his guides, listening and leaning on them to gain wisdom. This will increase his intuition and improve his life.

I thought, "How invaluable, this moment! This could be a turning point in his life!"

I asked what difference this would make to Rajan's life. It was revealed that this instruction would cause him to avoid making a lot of mistakes and also to cautiously make the right decisions.

We asked his Council, "What is Rajan's current life purpose?"

His Council answered, "Rajan needs to stop going through life alone, without his guides. He needs his guides!"

Rajan then told me that several years ago after his dad's passing, that this changed his life and set him on a spiritual course. What happened was like a miracle because Rajan started being curious about the afterlife. He really missed his dad and sought out mediums to try and connect.

Since his dad's passing, Rajan had often felt his dad's presence. One of those times, his dad told him telepathically, "Your future is outside India." This message felt like another miracle coming from his dad.

Rajan followed the advice and moved to America. He told me that he felt it was a great risk, going outside his home country, but when he moved, it worked out well. Now he tends to associate miracles when he feels his dad's presence, including instructions he's received, like moving to California.

The guidance was coming in strongly now:

- By being mindful and conscious of your guides, you'll be able to stop making careless and reckless decisions.
- In your past lives, you had things you needed to learn, and this was causing you to suffer.

This is why you weren't able to have happiness or to have the ability to enjoy your lives.

- To live a good life, you need to learn to be wise, alert, and responsible. Your guides will help you.

He explained that he now realizes he needs to control his impetuosity and to slow down and think things through before taking action. And, especially, listen to his guides!

He admitted that he frequently didn't use self-control to stop himself. He paused and asked for guidance here. They instructed him to learn to calm himself and to practice listening to his guides who are always with him. I loved how carefully he was listening and taking all the instruction to heart.

We asked another of his questions. "Why have I suffered so much in this current life?"

The guides explained that his suffering came from making quick decisions and not thinking through important issues. They told him to believe in himself and his capability and not try to do it another way such as taking a short cut. (Although they repeated themselves a lot, each time, it made the instructions even clearer. I could see him integrating the lesson.)

He'd been shown in both past lives that by not thinking through decisions nor using wisdom to discern his path, it led to danger and created a great deal of suffering, including the trauma of being murdered.

We had received the clear guidance that he mostly needs to establish a close bond with his guides and check with them often and follow their guidance. His guides will help him with all his needs – joy, happiness, success, protection, wisdom, and all blessings.

We asked his Council another question, "Will Rajan see his dad or his grandmother in this current life? Can he please have a sign showing when and if they show up?" (These are great questions!)

He was shown his guide wearing a miner's hat with a headlamp. The guide was looking for the streaming projection of lights in the dark sky of the universe. The guide says, "We are searching for them. We will help you. And someday when you meditate and listen to them, you will be able to hear the answer."

That was such a funny scene imaging his guides with miner hats while searching for his grandmother or dad!

It also revealed something deeper. It was being shown to Rajan to what extent his guides would go in order to be helpful. Putting on headlamps and going on a universal search revealed a deep level of caring interest in him!

Here's another of Rajan's questions. "Is my soul mate here?"

At first, when the answer came, Rajan didn't believe the answer. He was shown that his soul mate is a dear, long-time friend who lives a good distance away. She's from Serbia and they're close, as good friends, not lovers. They've had 3 past lives together. And, he was informed, that they will have another life together in the future.

"For what reason has she remained as a friend in this life?" They answered that he needs her, and they utilize each other through their friendship. He told me he misses her and wants to be with her.

She is his primary soul mate. He has a secondary soul mate but they said it wasn't important right now.

As we closed the session, we spoke about what had transpired. I asked Rajan, "On a scale of 1-10, how valuable has this Past Life Regression been for you?" He answered enthusiastically, "A 9 or 10!" (His energy had really picked up!)

I asked, "What did you most gain from it"? He learned that he needs to lean on his guides. And that in the past lives shown, he made crazy decisions, revealing that he needs to earn his success and not try to do a quick fix to meet his financial needs. He needs to meditate and listen to his guides and take their advice. Also, take time to slow down.

I asked, "To what extent do you understand yourself better as a result of the regression?"

He said that he could see that he had been acting like a teenager making all the wrong decisions. Now he's more mature and knows how much he needs his guides and that he needs to act responsibly.

He added that he's determined to do this. And, he reasoned, that this would be the way he would establish control of himself. He seemed happy and relieved. I believe he felt deeply comforted by knowing he was not alone and that his guides were with him *always*.

This is what I observed:

- It never ceases to amaze me that a person can be guided to my door to receive a past life that reveals the exact answer to their present life. And that this information gained from a regression, awakens them to stop making the same mistake, life after life. This is the power of just one regression! Time and time again, my clients leave with an overwhelming sense of gratitude and awe from the astounding significance of what happened and how it changed them. I'm so grateful!

- Rajan received the spiritual instruction very easily and even seemed to be in full agreement to begin with a practice of meditation and also to listen to his guides. He seemed excited to have these steps to take him more deeply into his best life. I could see him looking forward to it. Knowing he had guides and connecting with them was giving him joy.

- I'm aware of healing offered to new arrivals in Spirit World. They need restoration after a difficult life or from a traumatic death. But I had never encountered healing derived from streaming projections of lights. Another point that interested me is that he walked on the universe! No one can possibly anticipate what will happen in a Past Life Regression. It's profoundly fascinating.

- When we ended the regression, as with so many of my clients, they are both tired and in awe. I spent time after the regression, helping to review and decipher the information. Although I did this throughout the regression, there are much deeper levels that can occur the more you spend time with it afterwards. Always, transcribing the recording and reading it over and over, along with listening to your intuition, can help to deepen your Past Life Regression experience as well as your overall spirituality. I believe that the reason regression increases your spirituality is because it opens you. I've come to live in a state of spiritual openness. In this way, spirituality continues to pour in and be active.

Chapter 7

Love is What You Came Here to Learn and Protect

Soon after James arrived I could sense his deep spirituality.

An American, he was an avid student of ancient wisdom traditions and had been to India twice to pursue his spiritual studies even further. He was probably in his 50's, and well-dressed.

I asked what his intention for the regression was. He shared with me that he hoped to have clarity, insight, and guidance on the best path for his life.

During the interview, James explained that within the past couple years he'd come to the full realization of how much he had suffered from his dad's abuse, as well as his siblings and even the friends he'd grown up with.

As a result, 2 years ago, he moved across the country to San Diego. He was rebuilding his life, and today, he was interested in learning what would best serve his own evolution.

We dived in.

Bandits by the river

His past life opened on a beautiful, sunny day where he was taking in the beauty with great awe, standing outside in a full-length white covering, like a robe. (During the regression I wrote the word "beauty" many times. This was my cue that his soul is deeply appreciative of beauty and is one of James's gifts.)

Scene two, he was standing by a river facing a beautiful woman, and they were each realizing in that moment that they were "fully in love with each other." It felt like the awe he had been feeling in the earlier scene when he was standing outside taking in the beauty.

Just in this moment, they were interrupted by 5 to 7 men on the other side of the river. They were bandits on horses. Immediately, James realized that his job was to protect his sweetheart. He knew that they wanted to kidnap her.

He took her by the arm and they ran to a place nearby to hide, but James wasn't able to protect her against the men as he knew they'd kill both of them if he dared try. They captured his beloved. We moved on to his deep regret, and he reluctantly accepted the tragedy as unpreventable.

Crossing over from death, James moved very fast through a tunnel towards lights. When he came through the door at the end, he was in awe of the beauty.

In Spirit World James had a difficult time releasing the feeling of regret that he'd carried about not being able to protect his sweetheart. He floated in darkness, as he watched the past life move farther away. We asked for James's Spirit Guide to come for clarification about his journey.

Spirit Guide in Spirit World

Just then a large butterfly appeared and then turned into a male presence. This was his Spirit Guide and protector. James said, "I rely on him. There's no condition within our relationship."

James was informed that he's taken on many forms in his past lives. In all, he's had 1,200 past lives and later, we would learn that all 1,200 (including this one) were for one purpose, learning one main thing.

We asked his guide to please tell us for what purpose he'd been shown the past life with the beautiful woman in grave danger. The question was interrupted by something that came up for James to contemplate.

James began telling me that, in his present life, he gets bullied a lot. During his upbringing, people closest to him treated him disrespectfully, especially his father and siblings. Unfortunately, he realized that today he continues to allow others to do this to some extent. He explained that it's because of his childhood conditioning that he doesn't stand up for himself and that this is deeply ingrained. His Spirit Guide interjected, "Stand up for yourself in your career. You already know this. You wanted further clarity. Here it is." James thanked his guide.

The guide took James to a black door, wanting him to go through it to the other side. However, James was hesitant and preferred not to enter. Just then his butterfly guide put its insect arms around James saying, "When you're ready we'll go through the door together."

The door opened. They flew and arrived in a dark place. James could make out what looked like skyscraper buildings built with very precise geometric designs. And, he heard, "Welcome home!"

James had a confused look on his face. He said, "This is a learned place of knowledge. Not many beings are around, but some look like professors." James was being welcomed into a building. It was very dark and highly technical.

From this point on, and for much of the rest of the regression, he was told, "Don't worry about Shannon." (It turned out that James was being very modest about being shown his noble position here. He didn't want me to think he was arrogant.)

Council of Elders

They instructed him, "Just be who you are. Welcome home!" James was with his Council of Elders who were about 20 in number, seated on a long, huge rectangular shaped table. He sat across from them, facing the group.

There were 2 sections of the table. At the center and to the right of the center, there were 7 or 8 elders who were illuminated. To the left of the center of the table, about 15 elders acted as observers. They were not illuminated.

And there was something odd that caught his attention. There was an empty chair on the left of the center. James learned that this was *his* chair! Genuine tears of awe and gratitude spilled down his cheeks, learning that he himself was a member of his Council of Elders. We took a moment for him to take it in.

The Council said, "All of his lives, the whole thing, we're proud of you!" (again, James softly shed tears.)

When the elders were all laughing together, James exclaimed, "I know them!" They agreed and said, "Yes, you're one of us! Why do you think we brought you to Shannon?"

Then the Council delivered a message to James. "Love is real and the most awesome power of the universe. But, love needs boundaries, structure, guard rails, and it needs to be managed. Love needs to be protected!"

I asked James if this made sense to him. He said it did.

They responded, "That's it. You got it." James told me, "This is key."

I asked the Council, "Out of 1,200 lifetimes, is this what James has been mostly learning?" They implied, "Yes, and there are other lessons too. But this is the significant one."

This is what James has been learning for thousands of years. The Council said, "You wouldn't be one of us if it weren't for a very long time."

James' Crowning Moment in Spirit World

The Council said, referring to the chair arrangement they had brought to his attention, "James has been sitting on the left, next to the center, but now, after this life, he will be ready to move to the center right on his Council of Elders table, where he will interact with souls coming through. This meant that he would be sitting in the area among the illuminated elders!

The elders then reverted back to the message of all the past lives. They informed him, "This is what you had to learn: Love must be protected. When you go back to think about the life we showed you, know you should have protected her."

I asked, "But how could he have protected her?"

The council answered, "You could have used your ingenuity. All you did was run to the first place and hide. It was too close by. You should have used your intelligence. You could have found a better way to protect her. You were falling deep into love at the very moment the bandits were across the river. You were lost in love." They repeated it, "Lost in love." James was getting the lesson that he could have tried harder to be alert and make efforts to protect her - and their love.

The Council went on to explain how he could have protected her such as running around the hill, going to the boat on the river, or even doubling back to fool them.

James looked over at his butterfly guide. He said the insect's face was so awful. But the wings were so beautiful! James realized that when you consider the beauty of the butterfly you also realize that the beauty had to be protected by the structure of its solid body.

I sensed that the Elders were referring to James' beautiful character, full of love, and in need of being protected from bullying.

I asked if this was the main point of his 1,200 past lives. He indicated yes.

James was informed that he had now learned what he came to learn, and he would advance to the right of the Council's center where they were illuminated.

What an announcement!

This was the culmination of 1,200 lives, that, at that moment, was being announced as coming to a point of successful completion. And I got to witness it! I felt like jumping up and dancing. Upon reflection, I believe that James had already reached his grand life purpose from his many past lives. After a long process of study, reflection, and guidance from professional family counselors, he cut ties with toxic family members and friends. Although this occurred a couple years earlier, we were receiving the message of the impact this had on his present life as well. Mission accomplished.

James explained to me that he had been bullied all his life by everyone. That's why it was a lesson in this life. They told him, "You've had pain from not standing up for yourself. And now you learned to assert yourself." James teared up, saying, "I'm very humbled."

He thanked his guide and asked me to please let him be quietly alone as he completed his communication with them. The regression ended shortly after this.

I asked James, "On a scale of 1-10, where would you rank the importance or value of this regression?" James responded quickly and emphatically, "A 10!"

I asked James what he most gained from the regression.

He said, "Knowledge of my spirit. It was fantastic!" His soul had been on a long journey. And it meant a great deal for him to understand his status as a member of his Council of Elders. They told him, "You are living your life lesson. Stop self-effacing. Go and enjoy the rest of your life!"

James said it was a very powerful experience. And that hereon, and especially in his career, he'll be standing up for himself. He felt that regarding the term "protection," it was a seed they had planted, and he would let this seed grow. He would protect the awesome force of Love in the universe.

I asked, "In what ways will you do this?"

James said, "I'll be more self-protecting, self-confident, self-assertive, and self-assured. From now on, when I walk, I'll be looking up, unafraid to confront."

This is what I observed:

- I'm sure that in James' current life, he's received precious little empathy for his pain and suffering from being bullied. Imagine now, coming for a Past Life Regression, his pain was not only known and addressed, but advanced to healing. This is the power of a Past Life Regression!

- I was impressed how the Council repeatedly emphasized love as the most important force in the universe. And the wisdom of protecting it. It's of enormous interest to me that love would be so important and vast a lesson to his soul that it required an astounding number of lifetimes. And, although we often take love for granted, as well as its lessons, it shows how truly complex love is, how elusive its lessons for us all, and how vast an amount of time it takes to learn about love. Perhaps when we're dealing with a principle such as divine Love, we need to pause and realize the Angelic Realm we inhabit.

- Love was James's focus. It wasn't about a person or a relationship, though it may involve either.

- This regression caused me to believe that the lessons of love are the main lessons of our souls. And love is what we're here to learn. Afterall, love is what we all want and need. And it is, for most of us, the most important thing in our lives. So, of course, learning about love would involve an exorbitant, and perhaps an unimaginable, number of lifetimes. Consider the high reward, a seat at the Council of Elders. And not just a seat, but a seat lit by love. His 1,200 lifetimes had earned this high position!

- I witnessed a moment of historical and eternal importance as the result of James's last 1,200 lives where his soul gained the grand accomplishment of learning its main lesson. It was a celebrative moment of great and holy magnitude!

- As James was leaving, I asked if he was sufficiently alert from the regression in order to drive safely home. He said that he was fine and that he would be going by the grocery store on his way home. I told him to remember who he is as he was going to the grocery store. He is not just a human running an errand on his way home. He's an awakened soul who is part of his esteemed Council of Elders, and who has accomplished his life purpose.

Chapter 8

Overcoming Grief and Reconnecting with a Deceased Loved One

Amanda came early, eager to experience her first regression. I greeted her warmly. She was a tall and pretty redhead, over 40, and, as I would discover, quite articulate.

Unlike many who come for a regression, she hadn't studied the subject much or thought of it long before she called me. She came prompted by her intuition, which she always follows.

Although I didn't realize it at the time, I came to learn the great burden she carried from being true to herself while being opposed by others around her. This would occur in both her Past Life Regressions.

She explained that she lost her sweetheart, Mat, a few years earlier when he had a sudden heart attack. The jolt of his death left her feeling deeply grieved and somewhat guilty because she wasn't with him when he died.

She wondered if she could have prevented his death. "My sweetheart died within a few months of my Daddy whom I'd taken care of for a long time." She carried a lot of feelings of sadness, guilt, and loss over both these deaths of the two men in her life.

She wasn't sure why she came for a regression, except that she felt as though she was being guided to do it. She was open and curious. During the interview, Amanda shared that she had been a swimmer before she could even walk, and when she was 4 years old she participated in her first swim meet. She would later go on to qualify for the Olympics.

She explained that she's "all about water". Amanda took time to describe, in great depth, how much she loves being in the ocean or any water. And how wonderful it feels when she's floating or dwelling down at the bottom.

Amanda experienced two brief past lives.

Poor dirty orphan girl

The first past life opened in a scene somewhere in Europe in the 1400's. She described herself as a 12-year-old young orphan girl wearing a burlap dress to her knees. She was barefoot with muddy legs. Looking into an imaginary mirror, she saw dirty, matted hair.

She was trying desperately to hide and had found a temporary hiding place in a dark room. Her life was full of fear, always living in the terror that she would be found by adults who were looking for her. She'd been running from people when she got into trouble though she wasn't sure what the trouble was.

She described the disgust of the cold, wet, stone sidewalks and the filth everywhere. In the dark room, she could see mice scampering into the corners. She was cold. When she peeked out the door, she saw people walking on the paths, wearing brown, muted clothes. They were also very dirty and poor.

She transitioned to another past life.

Clean daughter with an impatient dad

The second past life opened and she was very opposite as a happy little girl, playing in a large field. The sun was warm and shining. She was alone, though she could see a dog down the hill, running and playing happily.

The little girl was clean and cute wearing a blue and white dress. Amanda said she was delighted to be clean in contrast to the previous past life.

In this life, she was about 7 years old with curly blonde hair. She felt happy and free. Her arms were spread out feeling the tall flowers. She commented that, "It's a large space." (This was one of her soul themes. She loved spaciousness.) She was laughing and enjoying the big dog who was running playfully.

Her dad was watching her. He was hoping she'd be finished soon with her play. He had a caring watchfulness, but he was also very impatient as he stood with his hands on his hips waiting for her. Amanda said, "He's always impatient with me."

Amanda explained that her dad wanted to work all of the time and he had no time for play. And even at times when he briefly played with her, she knew he would rather work instead.

Spirit World

That was the end of the very brief second past life. The next scene, she was in Spirit World. (In both past lives, she skipped a dying scene.)

In Spirit World, at first, she couldn't understand what had happened to her. She was floating in darkness. (This seemed strange, of course.)

It felt like she was in a huge space and that the darkness was holding her up. She sensed that she was in a space about the size of a large stadium. (I had already noted that her soul loved spaciousness.)

She could sense her long hair flowing around her head as it does when she's in the water. But this was very different since there was no water. Nor was she wet. Instead, it was darkness in which she floated. Amanda felt cocooned in this huge space. She said that the dark felt fluffy and she could float on her back.

She felt immensely comforted and began to cry when she realized that she had been to this place before. It was incredibly peaceful and seemed to meet a need for her to rest. I asked her if she was ready to meet someone but she explained that she needed time to rest in the dark before seeing someone.

It felt as though she wasn't alone, as though there was someone who was allowing her to float and relax. And she sensed that this individual was willing to wait as long as it took. In fact, time wasn't even an issue.

She sensed that, although she was in darkness, what was happening was something very good. And she was enjoying it. She felt restful while also being aware that someone was waiting for her. She was enjoying that there was no need for her to hurry. (Clearly, her soul needed rest and spaciousness, free of hurry. And darkness was providing this for her.)

Then Amanda became aware that there were people surrounding her inside this enormous stadium. She was floating in fluffy blackness at the bottom and it was filled with all these people watching her. The stadium may have been holding as many as 100,000 people. And they all seemed to be there for her.

She sensed a warm welcome from them.

Then she spoke about the mystery of how she was floating in this darkness. The dark continued to hold her and make her feel calm and supported.

Reuniting with Her Daddy

As she turned over and began floating in a forward direction, she felt excited, as though she was anticipating something good. She moved faster and instead of floating, she began swimming. And she had a warm feeling as she felt there was something around the corner waiting for her...

...Just then, Amanda burst into tears. She was deeply moved by what she saw.

It was her Daddy! He was telling her to relax and be calm. She was so happy to see him again since he passed away just a few years earlier. He said, "It's all okay." And he was also delighted to see her again! His smile was so big, and he looked much younger, appearing about 45 years old. He was laughing. It was a big and wonderful greeting.

Amanda saw 1,000's of people who filled the stadium. They'd all come to see her! They were smiling at her, welcoming, and loving her. It was wonderful! She said that she could remember this scene from before this time. The people were so happy to see her and she was overjoyed feeling their welcome.

She could hear their voices, but it sounded like a low rumble vibration. They weren't using words. But she heard words. (in Spirit World, we communicate telepathically.) Amanda expressed how good it felt to be back with them.

I asked for her Spirit Guide to come.

Spirit Guide

Amanda became aware of someone to her left. A presence. He appeared as a professor with black rimmed glasses, his hair parted and slicked back flat. He wore a sweater and she could see the top of his tie.

The Professor was with her standing with his hands behind his back, waiting patiently. Then, once he saw Amanda seeing him, he gave her his crooked smile. This is how she recognized him as her Spirit Guide. (Amanda was now smiling, amused, and happy to see the crooked smile again).

I asked, "For what reason is your Spirit Guide waiting?" She answered, "He's waiting for you, Shannon." I assumed that this was my cue to ask him questions.

I asked the Professor why he had shown Amanda the first past life when she was an orphan who was cold, damp, poor, and dirty. He explained that this was the past life where she was most scared. She was always afraid of doing wrong things and making a mess of everything. In that past life, she was alone.

The second past life, Amanda was the happy little girl on the hill, playing. But her dad (who she recognized as her Daddy in this present life) was always irritated with her saying there wasn't enough food or money and he had to always work. He scolded her because she was supposed to be taking care of the chickens.

The Professor said that the reason he showed her the two past lives is that he wanted to show her how "it gets better."

I asked what he meant.

Her Spirit Guide Professor said that, after each lifetime, she always sees him in the dark and learns that she's making good progress.

He comforted her and assured her that the life as the scared, dirty, poor little girl was the hardest one of all. He went on to explain why it was so hard for her. It was because Amanda didn't trust him and didn't understand him as her Spirit Guide.

Since the time when she was orphaned - a dirty, scared little girl - she had learned to come closer to him. And that explained the reason for her progress from a difficult life as a dirty orphan to a happier life as a clean little girl with a dad. That was the point the Professor wanted to make.

In her present life she's learned much faster to recognize her Spirit Guide Professor's crooked smile. This is what she's needed to learn all this time.

This meant that her life as the orphaned, dirty poor little girl would have been easier if she had understood to contact her Spirit Guide Professor for help.

And because she had learned to do this by recognizing his crooked smile, her subsequent lives had improved ever since. This is an important lesson for us all.

He wanted her to know that he'll always be here for her and that she needed to remember this place in Spirit World with her support from the dark, with all the people appreciating her, and himself as her Spirit Guide. They would always be with her.

He said to remember floating and how she felt relaxed and rested and how she can also find these feelings in the water and in the ocean. The ocean gave her the feeling of her soul in Spirit World, floating and restful and free. Amanda noted that the Spirit World scene was not heavy with burden, fear, or sadness, feelings so common in her present life.

Then a really big download came:

We were being shown the great value of her free spirit and playfulness. This also applied to her present life.

In Spirit World she loved floating in the dark. She reminded me of how much she loves sitting on the bottom of a pool, so quiet and with the water surrounding her. (It's fascinating to me how Spirit World created this for her!)

Here are words she used to describe her happiness as the girl on the hill: blissful, peaceful, comforted, where she belongs, without pain or weight or burden or fear.

She said that she thrives with this positive vibration. I asked if this was the description of her soul's vibration. She thought so.

I asked if this was also the purpose of her present life. She said it was. However, in her present life there's been a lot of opposition to her free ways. It seemed as though there was always someone telling her of their expectations for her and her need to conform to the rules, and to be like everyone else, as though she was doing things completely wrong.

She said, "I just want to be free. And this is all I need to do. I'm non-linear and I can't be confined. I need to feel happy and free." This statement rang with truth.

She commented on her Spirit Guide Professor who was standing there being so patient. Because of his patience, she felt incredibly free and never felt like she had to hurry. He told her to take her time and that it's okay to feel good. "There's no hurry and no need to do anything." (I felt her soul needed to know and feel this.)

She said that this freedom was in stark contrast to both of her dads - in both the past life and present one - who were inflexible and always rushing in a hurry.

The subject turned to Mat, her late sweetheart who greeted her lovingly in Spirit World. He spoke to her explaining that when they were together, he was always so impatient, always worried about work and this is why he had to die. (Amanda began to cry.)

He further explained that in his relationship with her, he couldn't be free like her and her freedom was why he loved her so much. She asked, "Couldn't you have learned how to be free?"

He said that now, in Spirit World, he feels free because of her free nature. Only now was he able to learn this. Now it's clear to him that he didn't have to always work or be so tense and worried.

She said that she had been a big influence on both her Daddy and Mat, as well as the dad in the past life, by her happy freedom and playfulness. She didn't fit into any box. She couldn't!

Amanda realized how much she needed to have spaciousness, freedom from hurry, and to feel clean. Floating helps her do this.

Floating was also her way of accessing deep rest. (I wondered perhaps if her soul needed deep rest in her present life because it required a great deal of energy to express its exuberant freedom, especially with all the people who surrounded her expressing opposition and judging her.)

She wondered about all the people in Spirit World who were watching her. Just then she burst into tears. She realized who the people were. They represented all the people who she has touched with her playfulness, joy, and the way she is naturally.

She even recognized many of the people individually. She said that some were people whose houses she used to clean. (Remember, cleanliness is very important to her soul!)

Some were elderly and had no one else to help them when she brought them food or took them on outings.

Now, all these people, in the 1,000's, were giving her a huge acknowledgment. This is why the Professor was standing over to the side, so she could see people acknowledging her and to know that she had helped them by being her natural, joyful, playful, loving self. She had forgotten that she had made all of them feel good.

(Amanda must have used the word "feel" 100 times!)

She said this is her life purpose and the reason she incarnates, to help people through expressing her playfulness, joy, lightness, and love. These people wanted to feel weightless, freedom, happiness, warmth, and enjoy the dog running. This is a high vibration she carries within herself and it influences others in positive ways. Learning this meant the world to Amanda!

It was now clear that she is not supposed to be stressed, impatient, unhappy, and scared. This is not her soul's contract. Instead, she's supposed to be herself, unafraid, free, and know that this is "good enough," regardless of criticism. She needs to always remember her true way of being, because this is her soul's gift to others.

She said that in recent years she had forgotten to be herself because she had experienced so much loss and sadness with the passing of Mat and her Daddy.

She saw how others need her gifts. Until now, she never knew that she had meant so much to so many people. It thrilled her. They were standing up on her behalf and thanking her. She had no idea that she added so much value to so many people.

As a result, Amanda said she'll no longer worry about people who are angry, jealous, or who judge her or tell her she's wrong for being a free spirit. Seeing the wide and far reaching influence she had on others changed everything. Now she knew her worth.

I asked, "What can you do now that you know this?" She answered, "I must keep being me." She added that perhaps other people are like Mat who don't realize her value until after they die. She realized she must be true to herself.

She continued, "Even if people think I'm crazy for being so playful and light, it's okay if I feel different from everyone else. My natural default position is bliss. I want everyone to be free. I must feel how big everything is – beauty, colors, and so much more than we see, think, or do every day. People can't see it because they're worried, impatience, and stressed to get something done or to get somewhere. They can't see water, birds, plants or the sun. Yet it's everywhere and it takes off all the weight. Stand there and see it. Feel how beautiful it is!"

The regression ended on this strong, happy note.

I asked Amanda what she most gained from the regression. And where would she rate its value on a scale between 1-10.

She said her biggest gain (and there were many) was feeling from Mat that he had to depart because he couldn't stop working or shake off his heavy load of stress and worry. And he realized, before he passed, that he wasn't going to get any better.

It also made her feel warm to recognize her Daddy as her dad in the second past life when she was the clean, happy little girl on the hill. She adored her Daddy and was thrilled to see him appear in her second past life. She knew his impatient ways but her love for him was stronger than his impatience.

I asked Amanda how she saw herself differently.

She said that the regression was an affirmation of who she is, the way she is, and the way she looks at things. This has real meaning to her today.

Amanda has suffered from people's complaints and judgments for not being "serious enough." And she's endured many outside forces telling her she needs to save money for retirement and to discuss a retirement plan and to conform to expected things in order to be regarded as mature.

Now she realizes that Mat died from being so serious, tense, worried, afraid, and from being buried in his work. He died instantly of a massive heart attack. She has carried guilt for not being there when he died and for not being able to prevent his sudden death. Now she realizes that it wasn't her fault and she couldn't have prevented it. She felt free.

She valued the regression at a 10.

This is what I observed:

- The regression gave a clear depiction of Amanda's soul. There were many adjectives to help her identify herself, such as: playful, light, loving, free, weightless, fearless, joyful, and taking in the bigness of beauty everywhere.

- The regression caused Amanda to realize her soul's need for floating, for the purpose of rest and for spaciousness to feel free. I sensed that being playful and light took a lot of her energy being on Earth where so many gravitational forces were working in opposition and where people are more likely to be considered as mature when they're stressed, worried, and afraid.

- It was incredibly gratifying for her to see the appreciation that so many people had for her soulful way that brings in love, lightness, and freedom. (She has received a lot of criticism in her present life for being this way.)

- At one point towards the end, Amanda told me she recognized many of the people in the stadium. She told me how she took care of people who had no one else and who needed companionship, someone to help them with food, errands, or getting out. It sounded as though her life was full of these people and of her generosity of giving. I had a feeling no one knew she did these wonderful things for others.

- Most people have no idea what their life purpose is. And they're surprised when it's revealed in a regression. With the surprise comes a depth of value to the person. Amanda's regression was full of lovely surprises: seeing her need for rest and play as a soul, the massive number of people acknowledging her gifts of bliss, and the explanation that Mat's departure meant that his life had completed when he realized he wasn't able to change from being tense and overly serious. This also brought the surprise that there was nothing more she could have done for him and she had given him the gift he most needed. Now, in Spirit World, he was more able to receive the gift.

- During our interview, I saw a pattern of her intuitiveness. She said, "Really? I haven't thought of that before." Then she went on to tell me that when she was 16 years old, a passenger in a jeep, she suddenly felt an urgent need to get out of the car immediately. Friends who were also in the jeep told her she was ridiculous. Still, she urgently persisted until the driver stopped and let her and her boyfriend out of the jeep. A few minutes later, after she had been dropped off, the jeep turned over in a ravine and one of her friends was seriously injured. I have a feeling that as Amanda contemplated everything she learned about herself that afternoon during her regression, she would feel the joy of full integration and deeply purposeful about accepting the way she is, knowing the amazing value she brings to others. This is one of the hardest things we have to learn –

accepting ourselves and being true to who we are.

- Because Amanda had a very short period in her past lives and most of the regression time was spent in Spirit World, this was an unintended Spirit World Regression.

- The next morning, Amanda sent me a text message saying, "Thank you so much for yesterday. I had incredible dreams all night and awoke with a profound sense of calm today."

Chapter 9

Self-Worth and Life Purpose Realized

When Dorothy wrote me to schedule a regression she explained, "I'm having a very hard time right now emotionally."

When she arrived, I felt the presence of a loving, warm, giving soul, although she appeared downcast, and looked deeply tired. For a woman in her mid-50's she looked youthful even through the heaviness she carried.

During the interview, Dorothy began to cry, saying she wasn't sure if she could be regressed.

She carried doubts about the regression and she went on to tell me that she recently learned that her husband of 30 years had been having a lengthy affair. She found his letters to his girlfriend and read some of their exchanges of passionate love for each other. She was heartbroken and distraught. Because of her distress she wasn't sure she could be regressed.

I felt compassion for her heartbreak and knew it was a turning point in her life. Yet I also wondered whether or not she was able to be regressed due to the overwhelming emotions, which might interfere.

Blocks like this are common when fear or trauma have someone paralyzed. It would mean facing the fear or trauma and all the feelings. This takes courage.

As we talked about her heartbreak, she became calmer and she decided to proceed.

The regression lasted about 2 hours. At least half of our time together was spent trying to lead her to a fully induced state. There were constant dead-end roads where nothing was happening. She was very blocked, which was understandable given her circumstances. I persisted in using a variety of techniques.

There were some false starts. In spite of her efforts, she just couldn't get past her blocks. Consciously, she wanted the regression, but her foot was on the brakes.

During one of the critical points, I asked her what was blocking her. She said that she was afraid. I asked her what she was afraid of. Tears flowed and she said that she was afraid of the truth.

I asked what truth she was most afraid of. More tears flowed as she said, "My life has no purpose." I assured her that her life had a purpose and that she had come today to find out what her purpose was and that, we would learn it together.

Finally, she was so fully regressed that she was almost asleep. I roused her gently and asked if she was ready to proceed with the regression. She said she wanted to sleep.

I gently and compassionately persisted and she said she was willing. I reminded her that whatever she was afraid of was small in comparison to the strength and courage it took for her to come here today and face what she most needed to face. I assured her that she could do it and that I was right there with her.

A scene appeared. It was a beautiful sunset over the ocean. The sun was not visible, but light came through the clouds, rippling on the ocean. Everything was midnight blue. She was taking it all in as she panned the entire scene.

I asked how it made her feel. She said it was calming. I knew that we had gone past the block. And the fact that she had seen herself peering out over this vast scene told me that she was now wide open. Her blocks were cleared. She had opened to more light.

I assumed that, from that point, we could go forward, but nothing was happening. She saw nothing. And, yet, I knew she was fully regressed. This is a predicament for the regressionist. I paused to send Reiki energy to the situation. I explained what I was doing. I also reached out in prayer for guidance.

Then, following my intuition, I opened a discussion with her, in her regressed state, to inquire about her life value.

She told me during the earlier interview that her 2 sons were grown. I said, "Tell me about your value as a mother."

Dorothy immediately became open and fluid as she discussed how deeply she loved her sons and how appreciative they were of her and how proud she was of them.

I affirmed the enormous value she had in their lives. She nodded. And it was clear she loved them and cared for them in every way, with total devotion for their entire lives. And, it had turned out well.

As a mother myself, I spoke of the endless sacrifices involved in mothering with love. She agreed. Her value as a mother had become self-evident to us both. This was the beginning of our guidance together in her regression.

Next, I felt guided to inquire about what kind of daughter she had been with her parents. Smiling, she told me that she had loved them deeply and they adored her and knew her immense value to them. She had been a wonderful daughter and her parents would agree. It had always been a happy relationship full of love. As she spoke, I felt the love settled within and upon her.

Then she volunteered how she had been devoted in her career and how much she gave to the job, just as she had given in every other area of her life. In her work, she had been generous in giving her time and honest efforts in return for her pay. She was clearly living with high integrity.

Normally in a regression, the client leads the regression and I take notes, asking questions along the way. However, in this regression, it was not being self-initiated by her, so it became necessary for me to lead in order for us to investigate her true-life value in these various areas.

Then it came time to inquire about what kind of wife she had been. It was the same beautiful story of how much she had loved and devoted herself and forgiven a million times.

She confessed that he had not been easy or even pleasant much of the time. She had lived with her husband's hot temper for many years. But, regardless of his behavior, she always did her best to love and care for him well.

I was now seeing Dorothy as a soul.

I pointed out that this is what her soul does. Because of the depth of her character, I considered her to be an old soul.

Considering how difficult a time we have learning lessons of wisdom in the human experience, it would require many lifetimes to build the depth and strength of her present character.

She was beginning to recognize at this point that her soul did carry great value and that this was significant.

The maturity of her character told me that she had to address and overcome many difficult obstacles, spanning many lives, in order to be so deep and generous within her soul. She was now starting to weigh this within her current life from the measurement of her soul's work, probably over many centuries, and perhaps even thousands of years. She had finally arrived!

We agreed that, regardless of outcomes, or if someone returned her love, still, she acted from her highest place because this is what her soul does. This represented her soul's standard.

I pointed out that it was obvious to me that she had contracted her current life to love. And that is exactly what she had been doing with her life. She agreed.

And, whether or not her husband returned her love had nothing to do with the sustaining value of her magnificent soul, rich with giving, making sacrifices, practicing patience and perseverance during hard times, contributing her light in ways of love and encouragement with deep, rich caring.

Her love is strong! She was now beginning to glimpse her true-life value and worth.

By comparison, we could see that her husband was still learning very basic lessons about love and still learning through failing.

Being a healer of many decades experience, I'm aware of how difficult a journey we are on and how many ways there are to fail ourselves and others. How impossible some of our problems seem to be and how easily we can talk ourselves out of doing the hard work of deep understanding of how to align with our soul's purpose of love and healing.

This is the plight of the human experience. Living consciously requires our constant alertness to detail and motivation and courage to learn how to comfort and encourage ourselves as we learn how to not give up when it's difficult, staying on the path of progress regarding our character and how we treat ourselves and others.

Dorothy explained that her husband had lied to her for 10 years. He had betrayed her, robbed her of a fair chance at their marriage, and allowed himself to excuse his behavior, even defend it, saying he felt it was his destiny to love this other woman, even inside his marriage with her. Pardoning his own deceit, living in lies, and feeling no remorse so easily spoke to his lack of integrity and their incompatibility of values.

It was interesting how, during her regressed state, we were guided to see her life from the objective standpoint of her behavior and how she had nurtured and loved her family to the best of her ability. This was turning out to be a review of her soul. She was passing with flying colors.

On the other hand, her husband had not stood up to his own responsibilities. He had failed himself, his wife, and even his lover. I think she began to see his betrayal was not her fault. And his behavior didn't cast a shadow on her self-worth or life purpose as his behavior was about his level of growth, not hers.

She could see from this perspective, for the first time, that it made sense that he must be a much younger soul than she. And she even intuited that a week before she came to the regression, wondering if it could be true but without understanding it. Now it was being reinforced. She remarked how she realized that she needed to rely more on her intuition. This seemed to be another message from the regression.

She could see that she had a lot of work to do to remind herself that she's a soul that gives love and has a purpose. And this is her life contract. It also became obvious that she needed to focus on loving herself more.

I commented that she has an angelic quality about her love, because her love is so pure and unconditional. I added that I imagined that others had called her an angel. She smiled and said "Yes, they have."

During the regression, she did not see a particular past life, but was cleared of any emotional block of blaming herself for the loss of her marriage, and she began to see the light at the end of the tunnel of the vast betrayal and heartbreak. She began to define herself as a soul, and in that vision, felt free.

As the session drew to a close when she was leaving, we hugged. I observed that her energy was lifted and much freer from the time she arrived, where she was tearful and petrified with fear and doubt about herself and the regression. She turned to walk away, then paused to ask when I was sending the recording of her session. She seemed eager to review again the amazing regression. Dorothy had gone to great depths and it required a tremendous amount of her energy to reach those places which would free her. She did it!

This is what I observed:

- Dorothy had a seismic paradigm shift. When she arrived, she held the belief that her life had no value or purpose. Her self-esteem was almost destroyed by the betrayal of her husband after reading his love letters where he poured out his heart of love for another woman when he had never spoken to her in this passionate way.

- Once she was introduced to the new paradigm of viewing herself as a soul, discovering that she was an old soul who was on a mission of love, and that she was accomplishing this goal successfully, it became less important that her husband rejected her for another woman. *His betrayal no longer carried the message of her worthlessness.*

- At the beginning of her regression, it looked impossible that she could be regressed. She was paralyzed by fear and doubt. And, yet, once she opened past the block, there was still no flow. As a regressionist, I felt guided to step in and, slowly help her to face the dreadful fear of having no life worth. Sometimes, the guidance comes through me. I feel it doesn't matter where it comes from, the guidance is always available. I am not the Source. But I allow myself to be used as a channel whenever necessary. And it seemed to be successful in addressing the main problem in her life and to enable her to go to a healing place with it. Sometimes clients aren't shown a past life. Instead, during her regression, Alice was able to connect with her Superconscious and she had a healing without going to a past life.

- During my years as a spiritual healer, I've found many women of great worth and soulful value who have married or partnered someone who led an unexamined life. It's the story of an advanced soul who partners a lost or unadvanced soul. And the advanced soul becomes influenced by their partner's uninformed opinions, turning the tables to throw blame on the more advanced soul. This silent mesmerism often occurs in close, intimate relationships. A partner can be a toxic influence! *Just because the person needs a scapegoat for their own deplorable behavior doesn't mean that the innocent one is to blame.*

- I recommend that wise souls on their path examine if their partner is also showing up at the mature levels of accepting responsibility to love, to give, to create peace, and to establish the relationship with fairness and empathy, while checking themselves on selfishness. Observation is the key.

PART 3
Spirit World Regressions

Chapter 10

A Destiny with Prosperity

Alexis was a beautiful, athletic woman in her early 40's. I sensed a willingness and openness about her, and she indicated that she was both curious and eager to get started with her Spirit World Regression.

During our interview I learned that Alexis had been struggling to achieve a breakthrough in her career for a long time. Although she had many significant talents and accomplishments, she had lingered in obscurity.

She expressed frustration that her meager income also didn't match her artistic abilities to produce great things, as she had achieved a lot for her clients but not for herself. She felt pained by constant setbacks that were also taking a toll on her health and energy.

As a result, Alexis had begun to doubt her value and lost confidence in her destiny. She indicated that she was ready to give up on many of her projects which she felt had held great promise. She passionately wanted to make an impact and leave a legacy and felt that time was wasting.

This was an important moment for her to have a Spirit World Regression and I shared her hope for helpful outcomes. Little did we know at the time that we were about to engage in a rip-roaring regression of epic proportions!

She experienced 4 in-depth past lives given during just one Spirit World Regression. This is unusual. Ordinarily I've seen that even one past life can suffice. However, my client's guides had an urgency to convey this information with a great deal of explanation about why her life has been so difficult and how soon she will be coming into the timing of her destiny. There were many insights given which offered Alexis great understanding of her soul – her character, talents, power, capability, and spiritual depth.

Past Life as a shaman

Her first past life opened seeing a moving train of elephants going by. In the front was a child to whom Alexis was yelling. Alexis was a brown skinned, dark haired barefoot girl, which she guessed to be between ages 3 and 5. She had arrived suddenly in the village alone, seeking safety. She had been lost in the jungle after being separated from her family and tribe.

Though immediately embraced by people of the village, Alexis had arrived to plea for urgent help for her own tribe. Something drastic had happened to them, but she couldn't speak the village language in order to make herself understood.

Alexis paused to comment about the wonderful tribal people who were overwhelmingly warm and friendly to her. They were a happy, harmonious, joyful people who sang songs all the time.

As we progressed, Alexis said that she felt her own tribe had been wiped out. A great loss. However, she was able to accept what had happened because of the immense love and acceptance shown to her by the village. She had nothing but gratitude to them for taking her in and adopting her as their own. They named her "The Different One."

I was impressed by how quickly Alexis adjusted to the loss of her people and her immediate, harmonious transition to a new tribe. This theme often comes up in past lives as something we incarnate to learn. She did it with ease. To me, this means that she has learned this valuable lesson of adaptation through previous lives.

Before coming to the village, she had been injured and walked with a limp. As they took her into the tribe, she spent a great deal of time working with the shaman who offered her healing, using herbs. She was eventually apprenticed to this shaman and did not marry or have children in this life.

In the next scene, she saw herself as white haired and very old. She was telling her story of survival to young children of the tribe as they sat around the fire. Alexis had learned their language. Now telling the children her story, she was seeking a successor to replace her as shaman.

In this scene as an old person, she was prophetic. She carried a heavy heart for her people for hardships she saw were to come and was worried about a big disease coming. She died with a heavy heart. (One of her soul qualities is a seer who carries concern for groups and for generations to come. These are often referred to as soul contracts. This is inlaid as part of destiny.)

We advanced to the day of her death. She was lying in a hut and the tribal people were giving her a sacred plant medicine tea to drink. She regarded the tea as a divine, intelligent being who would help her to die.

Everyone she loved was invited to be with her. She knew it was time to leave and her body was ready to go. Her spiritual maturity and acceptance she had of dying also revealed herself to be a soul of great understanding of its eternal nature.

Crossing over, Alexis found herself floating, rising like steam. Her spirit animal helpers from that life were encircling her: monkeys, elephants, jaguar, river dolphin, butterflies, hummingbirds. All the spirits to whom she prayed in that life were with her offering a grand send off. Everything was as it should be with unity, harmony, and gratitude.

Her indivisible connection with all of life – the plants, people, and animals – ran with extraordinary depth across time. This is certainly another quality of her soul, and a well-developed one.

She experienced no change in consciousness through death and transitioned seamlessly.

Spirit World

Coming into a bright space in front of her, there were white, gold, and silver colors of light. The great light felt like an embrace. This light represented beings offering her a warm welcome to assist her with re-integration.

It was very tranquil. There were 5 of them saying, "This is your home vibration. Peace. Peace. Peace. This is peace." (Alexis was being told that her home base is, not Earth or another planet or galaxy, but a vibration of peace.)

She found herself in a new vibration. She was greeted by hearing, "Well done! Mission accomplished!"

The angelic beings were a pure vibration of peace which would bring her into this same vibration. They changed her entire soul fabric.

Peace is one of the highest spiritual vibrations because it requires a great deal of learning and application of other strong qualities difficult to learn. Someone could spend entire lifetimes just refining the skill of patience, reconciliation, unity, and forgiveness which are only a few of the powerful qualities of peace.

I asked, "What was the purpose of the past life we just experienced in the jungle?"

It was explained that her past life was about pure resilience. She carries the signature of survival and also deep peace.

This was quite an accomplishment given all that she'd been through as a toddler who not only survived being alone in the jungle and was able to find help, but also she was able to rise to become a shaman, able of taking care of the entire tribe who had once saved her! I feel that she entered her Earth experience, ready to roll into her right place as a shaman in that life, even though it looked like it came out of tragedy from the loss of her tribe.

This is valuable spiritual insight because it's so common to ascribe a negative label – trauma, tragedy, crisis - to something that was very difficult and yet it turned out to be the right path for our soul.

They spoke, "Even though we are many, we are one vibration of peace, with profound excellence, majesty, ability, pure resonance of harmony, a portal of accessing light, and freedom from space, time, illusion or delusion."

(At this point she was spitting out words faster than I could write, all beautiful! I began to wonder if Alexis was an interplanetary being and that the peace vibration was her home base.)

I asked if this vibration of peace was her soul's place of origin.

She answered, "It's one of my home signatures. And a place where I'm invited to dwell for now." (The peace vibration was just one of her home signatures. I wondered how many other home signatures she bore. I also wondered if the peace vibration was key to her destiny.)

The peace vibration explained that she was always meant to come there. I noted the words "meant to" meaning this is part of her destiny package. "What else," I wondered, "was Alexis destined for?"

An ancient Greek king

Alexis interrupted herself to announce she thought that she was in another past life. This began her second past life.

Outside, she described the region as being near the ocean and having pine trees. She thought it was in or near Sparta. She said it was a Golden Age in ancient Greece. And Alexis was presiding as king.

Alexis discovered that she was presiding over the ceremony as the king in this past life. She's sitting on her marble throne, ruling the people and villages of the nation. I asked, "What do they call you?", hoping for a full name. She said, "They call me His Majesty."

She described herself as a powerful man with deep pride. As king, she helped her people create a time of great prosperity and abundance. (I felt that I was being given deep insight into her soul as one who takes care of others, even in large groups. This was what Alexis's longing had revealed in our interview – a desire to make an impacting contribution to others. She hoped this would be part of her current life's destiny. These are all clues.)

As king, Alexis had a big life of creating enormous prosperity for both herself and her people. There were a lot of animals – chickens and pigs and more, considered part of her wealth. She had conquered other tribes and took their gold, women, and animals. She even had ships! And, as she observed herself as king, she laughed saying, "I was a super ego!"

As king, Alexis enjoyed actualizing her power. It flowed through her veins during the festival, and she was filled with gratitude for all her accomplishments and the happiness of her people. Alexis could see her value and importance during this life.

This next scene opened showing the launching of her biggest ship to Egypt. There were one hundred rowers on each side of the massive ship.

As she said, laughing, "I created it all! The ship is going to Egypt and sending invitations to a meeting of the nations. She had a lot of honey (which I imagine was high value for bartering) and she oversaw the ships being loaded with her family and counselors all around her.

The mission to Egypt by the king's ship took longer than imagined. On her deathbed she was finally informed that her ship had returned, and her vision had been fulfilled for her country, and with a sense of completion she knew she could then die.

On Alexis' dying day, she was surrounded by her brothers, her wife, daughters and other family. They were all weeping.

Her only fear was for the stability of her nation and she felt sad. Her wife was a pure, devout, beautiful, faithful woman.

There was also a black dog with her in the room. (I mention the dog because in each of her 2 past lives, Alexis was deeply connected and strong with animal beings. It seemed natural that there would be an animal with her when dying.)

These were the golden years of her nation which she created and which were well remembered for immense prosperity and goodness. Her mission had been accomplished.

With a sense of peace after seeing that her funerary rites were completed as she had asked, she felt complete and simply drifted away.

Once she crossed over, Alexis was met by 3 guides. She laughed as they said, "You're a lot of work! Where do we begin with your ego!" They were very funny as they made their point and they were all laughing with her.

Guides love to use humor. This helps to lighten us up, which we often need following a past life. With our guides, there is only love and never scolding. When we mess up, it's often self-evident.

I asked, "For what reason were you shown this past life?"

It was explained that Alexis needed to remember the "felt sense" memory of having abundant prosperity, power, and ability, even though the past life was mixed with her big ego from that time.

Alexis's guides felt that she needed to feel abundance in her body through the energies of prosperity, power, dignity, and to also feel the power of abundance from what it was like sitting on the throne. Alexis commented, "It's giving me a rush in my body!"

I asked, "Where in your body do you most feel the rush?" She answered, "In my bones, muscles, and blood." (Her guides had given her an energetic infusion for prosperity.)

She quoted her guides telling her, "You can't manifest what you can't remember. She must remember this and not act without it." This gave her authority to create abundance in her current life.

Alexis explained that the 3 guides were imparting this so she could then go and act "as if" this abundance is still true for her. It was also their goal to lighten her up and lift her and help carry her to more prosperity. (Alexis had been carrying a heavy burden of financial pressure as a single mother.)

Note how help is available for you also. Her guides were working for her behind the scenes from another dimension, knowing full well the extent of her struggle, and giving her the assistance needed. This is good news for you, too, because you also have guides who are present to support you. Just remember to ask.

Following another past life, there was significant information given to Alexis by her Council of Elders regarding how her destiny and abundance are in progress. Here is an abbreviated version of this meeting.

Council of Elders

The elders poured out to Alexis many things that increased her understanding and gave her enormous comfort. Alexis arrived at the scene and described a U-shaped table with heavenly beings sitting around the table. She faced them sitting across from the table and her guides were behind her.

She described the environment as a temple - beautiful, spacious, airy, and with a stream of water running through.

Here is the beginning of things she learned from her Council.

- Regarding Earth, there's a new rainbow frequency coming in, "a vibration activation frequency." Through this frequency she will feel more nourished as she goes forward.

- They showed her a woman sitting in the dark balcony of a theater. This person symbolically represents Alexis. A spotlight appeared. And, when this spotlight shined on Alexis, she came out of the dark in order to sing her song. It was explained by the Council, "At that moment, you will know exactly what to do." Destiny has timing and order.

- They explained to her that she's been focusing on her many projects. However, she herself is the main attraction and not her projects. They told her that she's coming into the light even now and her frequency will be seen.

- They helped her to see that she's not been stuck. It's just that her higher frequency has not been available to her until now.

- They gave her an important message about herself. "There is nothing wrong with you!" (This was a vast relief because Alexis thought something was wrong with her since she's been unable to move into her right place in this life.)

I then asked the question that had brought Alexis to the regression, "How can Alexis be financially self-sufficient?" Their answer was surprising. She was told by the Council spokeswoman, who spoke emphatically, "Mark this for the next regression. It's a monastic past life. You took a vow of poverty."

What an uncovering! Was this "vow of poverty" what was acting as a block to her abundance now and holding her in bondage most of her life?

A Tibetan monk

Understanding that another regression would hold the key to unlocking her prosperity, Alexis returned a few days later for a second Spirit World Regression at the strong urging of her guide.

The past life revealed that she was a Tibetan monk who lived over 1,000 years ago. During this time, she went on a dangerous journey for her monastery, which necessitated crossing the Himalayas to India. The purpose of this dangerous rite of passage involved trusting the universe to provide for she and a few fellow monks who accompanied her.

Once they arrived in India, they lived on the streets and depended on the generosity of people who offered them food or sometimes took them in. These were people who also had little to spare.

During their stay, something very special occurred. A widower with no heirs gifted them with a large sum of money to take back to their monastery. This was wonderful news for the monks, who needed a new roof and other repairs.

Their journey home was perilous and difficult, and they arrived at their monastery exhausted and relieved to have survived.

Then arrived the moment of joy when Alexis could share the wonderful news of the special gift for the monastery. Alexis was grateful to be able to hand over the generous gift of the money.

But much to her horror, the important monk to whom Alexis gave the money, took the money and immediately threw it into the fire and burned all of it! This was the moment that would alter Alexis' life as a monk and would carry over for many future lives to come.

Alexis was upset and angry. The high ranking yet malicious teacher laughed. And he made sure to strip Alexis to the core saying that pride stood in the way of her spiritual path and that money is a distraction from enlightenment.

In this harsh, dramatic, even traumatic and wrongful teaching, Alexis was imprinted with a false teaching and a vow that would carry over to her present life.

Her vow against money meant that there should be no pride in accomplishment and her gifts would go unappreciated and she would even be tormented for them. (And this has followed her to this present day.)

Through the burning of money, Alexis learned to disavow money and material possessions in what she was taught would be in favor of her spiritual progress.

Now, hundreds of years later, Alexis's guide informed her that it was time to break the vow where she learned that money was bad and that it created pride and division.

It was amazing that this Council elder was present to give the full disclosure of what Alexis had been suffering from, unknowingly, for centuries. This shows our great need to stay close to our guides for instruction and healing.

She felt the entire regression made sense to her. It was meaningful how she's had thoughts of herself being blocked and limited as a person. And she had been taking it personally.

But they showed her how she had judged herself for being at fault as though she had done something wrong. Now she felt liberated.

She asked for a few silent moments to clear out remaining cobwebs and asked me to join by sending her Reiki energy. We did this.

I then asked, "On a scale between 1-10, what value would you assign to the Spirit World Regression?" She said, "A 10!"

I asked Alexis what she most gained from the Spirit World Regression. She said she had gained a lot of clarity, peace, and resolution. She commented on how real the entire Spirit World Regression was and how very mystical it was.

Here's what I observed:

- Alexis' past life as a king was a gift to her from her guides and teachers to help her carry the abundance essence, energies, and power which she needed in order to begin manifesting abundance in her current life. The understanding that this was her need canceled what she had been suffering from, blaming herself for being stuck and unable to manifest her career or to be able to make a large contribution to others.

- Seeing the king display a grandiose ego was entertaining. We both laughed a lot. However, the king also showed elements of her soul such as profuse generosity to his people. He also was creative, expansive, capable, powerful, and showed immense, caring leadership and high, unlimited responsibility as caretaker to his people. Here are some of her soul's characteristics and qualities that I observed.

- On Earth, she carries a very large bandwidth, holding watch over entire peoples and groups. Her soul is involved with caretaking.

- She's a seer who views beyond time and the present dimension to see higher vibrational energies and their value and the timing of them to activate.

- In 2 of the 3 past lives, she stayed after death to preside over her people to complete her duties to them and to her work. It showed a massive amount of love and sense of extraordinary responsibility, dedication, and commitment.

- As a shaman and king and monk, Alexis was involved with a community of people. She said that since being a teenager, she's been looking for her tribe. This is part of the destiny she has been waiting to fall into place. And she's sensed this for a long time, now confirmed by her Council.

Chapter 11

An Interplanetary Soul and A Spirit Guide in Training

When I greeted Connie, I immediately connected with her smile. She was an Asian American in her early 60's and eager to experience a Spirit World Regression. We each could hardly wait to get started!

I quickly learned during the interview that Connie had many people in her life that she wanted to know about.

Connie's main concerns were to know if she owed or had further obligation to her two husbands, one deceased and the other, her ex-husband.

She also needed to know if her son's disability was the result of something she had done. I learned as the afternoon went on that relationship contracts were extremely important to her.

She also shared with me that she had a rare disease and wanted to know if it served a purpose in her life.

I was impressed that Connie had little fear, a lot of curiosity, and was eager to check her responsibilities to others.

She shared with me dreams she had since childhood of floating on a cloud as well as being in Atlantis when it fell. She felt these may somehow be past lives.

A wedding day and great wealth

The first past life opened on her wedding day. She was dancing with her husband to the live orchestra playing in their mansion's ballroom. They were immersed in opulence. Upstairs her personal maid waited for her.

Connie commented that her maid was kind and looked after her. Outside, there were 10 riding horses housed in their stables. Many servants everywhere were serving the finest and best to their many guests. She was smiling broadly as she described her happiness and the wonderful time she was having.

Later, in the regression, it would come out that her happiness and wealth would end. It was deep south 1849 and she would lose her husband during the Civil War. She would also lose all her material possessions and even suffer great abuse, including physical beatings, from her husband's greedy family members. The past life scenes ended there.

Nepalese monk

The second past life opened with Connie as an 18 year old boy, ringing the gong of his temple in Nepal. The gong was announcing a ceremony. She was living at the monastery and would soon become a monk. Her name was Shenwa.

As a monk, she went to classes and practiced Buddhism. She loved it. Her parents sent her there. It was around the year 1500. It was a special privilege to be the gong ringer at the monastery. She studied hard, exercised, and followed the rules. Her path was to help people to reach nirvana and her personal goal was to become enlightened.

Spear hunter for the village

We then quickly moved to a third past life. (I never know in advance where the regression is taking my client. In both of the past lives, I asked Connie if she was ready to advance to the next scene in her important past life and she indicated she was. Then, without any notice, we would find ourselves in yet another past life.)

The third past life opened with Connie as a 20-year-old black African man in the jungle, hunting for food, along with 5 elders from their village. It was their responsibility to bring in all the food for the village. Her position as the spear hunter made her family proud.

Spirit World

As I was setting her up to go to the next scene, Connie announced that she was now in the clouds. She bypassed the death scene and moved into Spirit World.

I asked what had happened to the spear hunter. She said that he was brutally murdered in an attack against the village. He left behind a 9 year old son, crying. (Connie recognized the crying son as her current son, who's disabled.)

Connie was now relaxing and floating in Spirit World. She said that, although there were no sounds, there was a low vibration hum which helped her to stay in the White Light. The light made her feel well and feel free.

Effortlessly, her Spirit Guide appeared. She called him "Charlie" and told me that through intuition, she'd been aware of Charlie since her childhood. He causes her to feel calm and patient. Connie was wearing a huge smile now.

She also had 2 additional guides, but she was told to pick just one. Charlie became her main guide.

Charlie wanted to take her somewhere. He became a light in front of her and they moved together going very fast through the clouds. She found that she could jump to the clouds and it would help her move faster.

Connie's work in Spirit World

Her guide took her to a cave and he waited outside. Inside the cave she discovered she was in a beautiful temple, a holy place. I asked Connie if she had entered another past life or was this located in Spirit World. She answered that she was still in Spirit World.

The temple was huge, had very high ceilings and was completely bare. She was alone but then monks in brown and white robes appeared. She realized that she was inside a monastery-type structure.

I asked her to please describe what goes on in the temple. Connie said they were teaching the monks how to use the mind to govern the body and also how to make the body strong. It was her home. This is Connie's soul work when she's in Spirit World. I was eager to learn more.

I asked if she was a Spirit Guide. She answered that she was not. I asked, "Are you a Spirit Guide in training?" She answered, "I am!"

I asked, "What do you do in the temple?" She indicated that she followed the orders of the Council.

Council of Elders

Her Spirit Guide then took Connie to her Council of Elders. They were 7 older men and she recognized her dad as one of them. As they looked at her, she kept her eyes down out of respect for them. Standing around her in a circle, they wore white robes and there was great light everywhere surrounding them.

One of the elders identified himself as Leo, the spokesperson. He asked, "Why are you here?" At this point, we brought out her questions.

We asked about the first past life and for what purpose she was shown the past life as the bride celebrating her wedding day whose husband died and she had to live with his abusive family.

Leo explained that there's a lot of both happiness and sadness. She was happy for only a short time before the war came and then she lost everything. She endured devastating losses due to her new family members' greed, arguing, and violent abuse against her.

I asked for what purpose this occurred. Leo said because of her efforts to overcome pain from this past life her current life was much easier. Leo added that she learned not to fear violence and to trust that all would be well.

Connie began putting things together privately. She was shown the purpose of many of her most significant relationships and their importance to her soul.

She said that in the first past life when the newly wed husband died early and left her with the abusive family, she was being shown that he owed her because they had married for life and he had broken their contract from an early death. Their contract was to work together to help each other become better individuals.

We moved on to inquire about the second past life when she was a young Buddhist training to become a monk.

She shared that this life was very happy because she was on her soul path. And this is the practice she has in Spirit World, so she felt happy to be aligned with the work of her soul. She loved helping others and living with a pure heart.

We asked about her third past life and for what purpose she was shown herself as a spear hunter who died leaving behind a son crying.

It was revealed that this life was shown to her because of her present life's son. In this third past life she left her son before having time to teach him in the higher ways.

As a spiritual teacher, her soul teaches enlightenment and helps people to attain it. Since she was unable to complete her son's training on the path of holiness, he was sent to her again in her present life. It was unfinished business.

I asked how it was going with her current son and his disability. Was she able to teach him? She indicated it was going well and she is helping him.

We asked Leo if her son was fulfilling his purpose in this life. Leo answered that he was.

We then asked Leo how Connie was doing in her current life. Leo answered, "You could help more people." We asked how Connie needs to do this. Leo said to listen, give good advice, and wish them well. Leo emphasized that she needs to always wish them well.

It was explained that part of her Spirit Guide training would involve more incarnations. But for now, she knows all that she needs to know.

We asked about her health. They answered, "Your health is part of the program." It was explained that her health condition necessitated that she work to overcome her physical challenges.

But at the same time, she needs to be willing to do the work to help others. This is a condition of her contract here. They further advised to help family and strangers and the people she comes across. In the flow of her life will be the people who she will need to help.

We continued to ask from her list of questions brought to the session.

We asked for what purpose did Roger, her late husband, pass on? This is the father of her son. Connie's Spirit Guide explained that when her husband died, all was finished and complete. He indicated, "Life goes on. This is important."

From her present life, we asked about her baby, Janet, who died a few days after Connie gave birth. Her disabled son reports that he often sees her. It was explained that Janet is assigned to her son. When he calls on her, she comes to help.

We asked to know more about her role in Spirit World when it was shown that she ran the monastery at the temple.

She was in charge of souls and taught them to train their minds to heal their bodies. We asked, "How was this done?"

It was explained that a pure motive makes the mind strong so it can direct the body. For the soul to provide healing, it must be caring. Healing begins with the heart's pure intention. In order to train their minds and be helpful to themselves and others, they learn to purify their desires.

They were also taught the importance of completing a relationship, and to part in peace. The goal is to be one. Integration, not separation. This is the mission.

Life as an interplanetary soul

I asked if Connie is an Earth-based soul.

In response, her Spirit Guide, Charlie, wanted to take her to a place outside of our galaxy, a water realm, a "place of great waters."

Connie commented that she remembers being there before. This is the home of her soul where she most likely incarnates.

If you're an Earth-based soul, you mostly incarnate to Earth. If you're an interplanetary soul, you most likely incarnate from your home planet or interdimensional dwelling to Earth as well as other locations.

Here was our answer: Connie was an interplanetary soul!

She went on to explain that on her soul planet, souls can go in and out of the water as well as walk on the water. There are no ripples and no fear of the depth. The water cannot cause any harm. Everyone lives in the water, including herself. There is also some land, quite level. There's no talking, only telepathic knowing.

I asked what she ate on the water-based planet? She said that there's no food. They took liquid nourishment and it was available for everyone in abundance.

I asked how it felt to be there. She said it felt light. There's no weight, no gravity. Everyone floats on the water and even outside the water. She could go to the water's surface and jump all the way to the clouds and be playful and happy.

I asked what her soul did on this planet. She answered that expressing peace and being peaceful were the main things.

She came to Earth from this water-based home planet. There was no name given to the planet. She's had thousands of lives on Earth. Connie commented that mankind hasn't changed in all their years on Earth. They still have many attachments to greed, personal power, and harmful passions.

We continued to discuss a few more of her relationships and their contracts, as well as her main role of keeping peace and being a spiritual teacher. Then the session ended.

In conclusion, I asked what she most gained from the session.

Connie said that since childhood, she had a great fear of violence. Now she understood where it came from, when she re-experienced the trauma of being violently murdered by enemies of the village when she was a spear hunter. I was grateful that this trauma, carried over into her present life, was finally released.

I asked Connie what she had learned about her soul. She said the regression confirmed as true the following:

- She always wants to do her best
- Memories and dreams about playing in clouds and being in Atlantis
- Being in a monastery
- Being brutally killed

I commented at the end that I saw her soul with some of the following qualities and gifts:

- Devotion to her spiritual work and to nirvana and enlightenment
- Pureness of heart
- Being a spiritual teacher as well as a learner
- Being a guide who knows the path of wisdom and the necessity of patience in helping others
- Being a devoted, serious worker who holds herself highly responsible to her life purpose

Connie clearly understood that the soul's learning is accomplished through many lifetimes and not through just one life.

This is what I observed:

- Connie is a soul who is clearly on her path with determination and focus on success. She held herself to high and strict standards to help others, be patient, and complete her relationships with peace and oneness as well as to live with a pure heart and to learn as much as she could. Her spiritual strength of character was deeply impressive.

- As a regressionist, I was grateful she connected with her Spirit Guide, her Council of Elders, and saw that her dad was on her Council (I consider that big news), and learned that she was a Spirit Guide in training (a big piece of information that accounts for her seriousness about being in alignment with the purpose of her many lives).

- She was able to make many discoveries including that she is an interplanetary soul and not an Earth-based soul. It was also meaningful that she now understood her dreams about clouds since her home planet is all about water and clouds.

- One of the top reasons she had the regression was to learn if she was living up to her soul contracts on Earth. This was confirmed.

- Also, many things she thought since her youth were confirmed, including that Charlie was her Spirit Guide and that she'd lived in Atlantis.

- I noted that Connie is a soul who is seriously focused on her soul work and not easily distracted. She expressed little to no emotion. In fact, no tears were shed, which is unusual during a regression.

- It was empowering for Connie to learn so much about her soul during this one regression. At the end, I asked the question, on a scale between 1-10, where would you rate your regression and the impact it had on your life?" She laughed and said, "Of course, a 10!"

Chapter 12

A Light Worker
from the Angelic Realm

Melinda arrived happy and eager. She's had 10 previous regressions, but it had been a few years since her last one. She's a vibrant and playful grandmother with a quiet voice, and a deep sense of her spirituality.

During her interview, she shared that she had just recently come to realize how fearful she had become and how much suffering this had created for herself and others close to her.

She expressed frustration and discomfort around the strong fear that was driving her need to control everything on a daily basis.

It was becoming increasingly hard for her to trust that anything would work out well without her interjecting her control. She realized that she'd been doing this for decades, but lately it caused her to see the enormous stress this imposed on her life and others around her.

In addition, Melinda also wanted to know her life purpose.

During our session, Melinda had several past lives shown to her. None of them went to completion. However, we paid attention to what they were showing us.

Hidden gold

The first past life imaged Melinda alone, outside. She was afraid and hiding in the dark. It was the Victorian period and she was in her 20's, dressed in a beautiful, fancy all-white dress. She was standing, looking at a building in the distance.

In the next scene she realized that the building was a church. Others were entering. Melinda entered the dark church's basement. She carried a candle as she looked for something. She discovered a sack of gold coins. They were lit up by her candle, but they were also glowing by their own light. She was terrified by this.

It seemed to me that Melinda was stuck in her regression. We weren't able to advance past the darkness, fear, and efforts to complete a scene.

I deepened her by turning to her breath and asking her to relax. We continued.

I asked Melinda where in her body she was holding her fear. She answered it was in her solar plexus. I asked her to please tell me what color the fear was. It was black. I asked, "What color does the black need in order to be cleared?" Melinda answered, "Deep, vibrant cobalt blue."

I explained that the vibrancy of the color had the power to dissolve the black and to replace it. And as the blue entered her solar plexus, she would feel the black leave.

This exercise worked. The black left her body and was replaced by the cobalt blue. A white light then took over the blue and filled her entire solar plexus, making her feel safe and secure.

I asked Melinda to join me inviting her Spirit Guide.

Spirit World

Archangel Gabriel immediately appeared.

I asked Gabriel, "Is Melinda of the Angelic Realm?" He answered, "Yes."

He explained that she's of such a pure consciousness that it's very difficult for her on Earth. She's pure light and love operating on Earth where it's very violent, judgmental, and hard to manage.

Archangel Gabriel explained to us that Melinda had a tendency to hide. Earth's energy could be strong, difficult, and hurtful. And, as an empath, she felt this deeply. Managing her feelings and trying to prevent herself from being overwhelmed took a lot of time.

As a result, she felt continually tossed around, afraid, unable to get her bearings, and without any control. We saw immediately that this was the source of her extreme controlling impulses. We continued on.

I asked if Gabriel was her main Spirit Guide or if Melinda had other guides. Gabriel answered that, although she had other guides, he was her main guide. He explained that he's always here for her but that she's been afraid to act on his messages to her.

I asked about Melinda's purpose on Earth. He told us that Melinda brings the childlike light into the world. It has purity and is greatly needed in the world. This purity is her essence. But, he explained, Melinda was having a hard time staying grounded in her essence. She was afraid to stand in it.

She told me that she was aware of this and she fears that by standing in her light, she won't be strong. She feared that if she revealed completely who she was and what she'd come to Earth to share, that the world would laugh at her.

Melinda continued speaking from her Super conscious. She's terrified of being judged. She worries constantly about being accepted and struggles with how to convey her essence on Earth.

She explained that her controlling issues don't represent who she is but it's her way of coping. We were gaining a lot of insight.

Gabriel joined in and explained that Melinda knows she needs to let go of her fear and to trust being who she is. But she explained that she hides because there's so much judgment in the world and she's terrified of being judged. It was as though there were two conversations going on – hers and Gabriel's - and only Gabriel heard them both.

I asked Gabriel, "What would happen if Melinda would come forward and be herself fully? What's the worst that could happen?"

She quickly answered, "I would shrivel and die and completely disappear!" Tears were flowing. I could see that the terror was like a toxin, preventing her from being seen under any circumstances. Her life purpose had become one of needing to be successful at hiding and trying to cope with the possibility that she would be found out and judged.

I asked Gabriel to please step in and help Melinda. He said that she has to remember who she is and what she came here to share. This is her life purpose.

I asked, "What is your role in the Angelic Realm?"

Gabriel said that, as a childlike light, she's connected with the babies in the Angelic Realm. Her role is to see them in their pure essence of their purity, which helps them to remember what a gift they are as they prepare for their journey to Earth.

I asked, "Is Melinda successful doing this in the Angelic Realm?" Gabriel answered, "Yes, because she understands what it is. It's her soul essence as well so that's why she can do it. And she knows how hard it is to hold onto the pure essence while on Earth.

I asked Gabriel, "How can Melinda fulfill her Earth mission?"

He answered, "Return to your child center because your natural interests come from that place. Expressing yourself from the center of your childlike light is what's missing in your life. She keeps pushing it away and becomes disconnected from herself. We all have gifts. But if we don't share those gifts of light, they don't get given."

I asked Gabriel, "How can Melinda give her gift of light? Can you help her?"

He told us that Melinda has to be strong and have courage in order to move away from her timidity. He explained that Melinda's inner light communicates to her and she hears the messages, but she's been afraid to act. She needs to focus only on the messages and just be and do what she's being shown.

The problem arises when she thinks of her essence coming into the world and fears being judged and worries about how she'll be received. This seemed to be terrifying to her.

It was explained that she must ignore the discomfort and walk through it.

He said that he's always messaging to her in spite of her fear and discomfort. He said, "We're here for her and supporting her life purpose on Earth to be her unique light. Her purpose is to be her light. In this way, many other lights now who are having similar challenges, will be helped."

He continued, "She must walk past timidity and stand in courage." I felt that as he was giving her this message that he was also infusing courage within her.

I asked about her troubling control issues. Gabriel explained that her controlling issues are from her fear. He told her to feel the fear and express her light anyway. He advised, "Trust that this is her life purpose and to express this in all its different forms."

I asked what forms he was referring to?

Gabriel explained, "Her childlike light emits through forms such as art, music, and writing. Her soul is within these. These are good channels for her childlike light."

I asked Gabriel if he had any other important messages for us.

He answered that family was a very important connection for Melinda. "Being her authentic self is a key factor and her desire to be a light in her family will come through her authentic self, versus hiding herself. She must let herself be seen. And she will be okay."

I asked, "How is it she'll be okay by letting her authentic self be seen?"

Gabriel explained that she needs to let go of all self-judgment.

I asked if Melinda had incarnated before from the Angelic Realm.

He answered, "Yes, 40 lifetimes. Each time she comes here, she learns more.

There's also a balance aspect. With some of her lifetimes her personal expressions have dominated her life and she didn't have to balance family and relationships.

However, in this life, she's swung to the other side and she's lost her personal expression. Now she's finding the balance. She needs to stop continually looking outside herself for courage and begin coming from within herself."

He explained that going to her quiet place is necessary to support her endeavors because she won't receive her courage from outside herself. It comes only from within.

At this point, Melinda began crying. She explained, "My fear is so great that I feel it's impossible!" She wondered why it was so hard.

I asked Gabriel, "How can it become easier for Melinda to express herself outside the fear?"

He answered, "She needs to remember to self-parent herself. Imagine what she would be saying to herself if she was her own parent, knowing how much she loved and encouraged her child and for her child to become all it needed to be. Remember that we're part of God and imagine how that love feels."

He reminded her that she's not alone. There are so many souls on Earth who have a hard time being able to express themselves. She's been teaching this to Angelic Realm babies. Now she must offer this same loving support to herself.

Melinda said, "I want to be my real, authentic light and to express my true self!"

I asked if she had energetic blocks in her chakras. It was explained that her energy blocks were from not expressing her true self. She needs to express her authentic self in order for her light to emit.

When she's emitting her light she acknowledged she felt lightness, connection to her passion, freedom, a noticeable lack of focus on others, an easier time letting go, and more flow.

I asked what are the qualities that appear when she's not emitting her light. She said there would be: no passion, no spark, dullness, heaviness, and a lot of negative emotions such as resentment anger, frustration, lack of joy, and even indigestion.

As we ended, I asked how she felt about the regression.

She said it was confirming of many of the things she's intuited and now she needs to trust all that Gabriel was messaging to her. She reiterated that she needs to disallow fear and not allow it to prevent her from being her own support system. She realized that no one could do it for her.

She said she gained a deeper understanding of the importance of emitting her childlike light and that she realized she needs to express it else it will be a deep loss. She calculated the loss of years from not being connected to her passions which would have allowed her light to shine.

She wrote afterwards that what Gabriel revealed was what she's been shown about herself her entire adult life. And she deeply appreciated the reminder to let her angelic love shine forth in all things every day.

Here's what I observed:

- Melinda is in her 60's. This crystal-clear regression was like a read-out of her life story and how difficult it has been struggling with the fear of judgment and even judging herself. But also, how magnificent a soul she is and how it longs to shine.

- I had a feeling before the regression that she was an angelic being. Even though her light hasn't emitted at the magnitude she wants or needs for her life purpose, I can tell you that by knowing her, I have viewed and felt her as an angel, for sure. And I'm sure I'm not the only one. I thought, "I wonder how much more we all stand to be showered by her greater light!" I hoped she would find a way to lean on inner strength and courage in order to overcome her fear.

- Once we got through the brief past lives, which never went to completion, the vast majority of the regression was spiritual where we gathered a great deal of vital information about her soul and her life purpose. This takes a lot of time. These are the moments I live for as a regressionist. What could be more important than learning who you are, where you come from, and what you're doing here. And even to discover that you're from an Angelic Realm as a caretaker of babies who are also childlike lights! And her work is to see them, encourage them, and love them! These discoveries are magnificent to learn! It didn't seem necessary to ask for what purpose she was taken to those past lives. But on hindsight, it seemed logical that, in the past lives, the buildings she feared, most likely, were her true visible self on Earth. And the hidden shining gold coins in the basement represented herself deeply hiding her light.

- This regression could be life changing for Melinda. Having a one-on-one talk with your archangel has a great deal of power and influence. This is the type of regression that will have long-lasting effects.

- Melinda's regression reminds us of the enormous courage required in order to express our true selves. This rite of passage can feel like a treacherous crossing over a swinging bridge with roaring wild waters raging below. Everything's at stake and it's a long fall. But considering also what's at stake when we succeed, the journey is more than worth it. By trying, little by little, our efforts teach us better ways of expressing our soul on Earth. Each one of us must take this journey, sooner or later. We can appreciate when we see someone on their journey to be so daring as to express their true self. We can extend our respect for their sacred undertaking. The healing power of expressing our true selves causes my heart to soar to no end!

- Once you see your true self, something happens where it expands into a kind of blissful fulfillment. Then find another layer surfaces that wants to also come forward into expression. This becomes the journey of your soul.

Chapter 13

A Soul of Infinite Possibilities

Lynn was a 33-year-old woman, visiting from out of state. She arrived with an eagerness to learn about her soul and she also wanted to know about her life purpose and what she could do to better fulfill it.

There was another interest as well. Lynn hoped she could meet with 3 loved ones who'd passed on, including her dad, from whom she had suffered great grief.

Native American crossing the wilderness

An astonishing past life appeared. The first scene revealed that she was a woman wearing hides, tracking an animal.

As she stopped to drink water from a stream, she saw people on the other side of the bank. As she watched them while hiding herself, she noticed they made clanging sounds. Lynn identified them as white men, and she sensed that they weren't friendly. She didn't trust them.

She immediately turned to go home as this was important news for her tribe. She said she could feel her adrenalin flowing. As she turned to quickly leave, she could hear the white men's scouts close behind, though they hadn't seen her.

As she fled back to her camp, and as she grabbed the children, they could see the hairs on her arms standing up. She had an overwhelming sense of doom and felt she'd gone from being a hunter to a prey. Her nerves felt as though they were on fire.

Just then a storm broke and as they fled, she was delighted because it meant they couldn't track her and her family. Their journey ahead was long and hard. Every time one of her scouts went back to check, they had to keep moving as the white man was close behind.

She commented, as they travelled, that she knew the white man consumed the land at a ferocious rate, yet they weren't aware of it nor sensitive to what they were doing. They were hundreds in number, spreading like fire across the field. And she sensed thousands more behind as they were looking to take the trees as firewood. Lynn knew she and her people could never go back.

They eventually joined another tribe. Sitting in the lodge with the elders, Lynn spoke about what she'd seen. Some didn't believe that the white man was a threat to them.

Regardless of their opinions, Lynn had a strong knowing that her people had to keep moving. The tribe who had sheltered them stayed behind.

On the journey, she had a vision of a craggy mountain pass and she instantly knew that it was the only safe place for them, so they headed there. (Consider that she was only following a vision. There was no actual confirmation that such a place existed. Nor was there a map.)

As they migrated, the snow fell and over time, their numbers from the original 18 thinned. They were a happy family and now a small, tight knit group. They continued moving for years and finally arrived at the Pacific Ocean where she felt safe for the time being. Another tribe greeted them, and she felt they were surrounded by good company. She recognized how far they'd come.

Finally, Lynn and her people arrived at the craggy mountain she'd envisioned. She described it as, "a good and sacred place with secret caves." After all their travels, after traveling for years, they had finally arrived at their destination! Lynn told me that at this sacred place, they would gather wisdom like a raven gathers shiny rocks.

Her tribe identified themselves as "keepers" of memories, herbs, stones, time, and all things precious. It was the northwest mountains, perhaps in Canada or Alaska.

Part of their tribal sharing was to gather and tell stories. She said there were about 12 of them remaining, living in the heart of the mountain.

We went to her last day of that life. She said she was about 100 years old.

In her last hour, she climbed a mountain, feeling the wind and looking out at the view. She knew it would be the last time she would climb the mountain. As she climbed down, she felt the cool stones beneath her feet, the wind, birds, trees, and the green that soothed her.

She was greeted as she returned from the mountain, surrounded by loved ones who gave her broth, warmth, and love. She was grateful she'd survived the epic journey as she went back over her stories to be sure she'd told them all.

Then she died peacefully.

When she passed on, she sank down into the stone beneath her body, then sank deeper into the mountain. Next, she transformed herself into the mountain and she became the bird soaring around it. She became the trees she'd said farewell to earlier. She had no sense of disconnection or separation. Lynn told me that she soared with the eagle and her path was complete.

We asked for her Spirit Guide to come forward.

Spirit World

Her guide called himself Great Wolf. He was the biggest wolf she'd ever seen and she described him having very green eyes.

We asked for what purpose she had been shown that particular past life. Great Wolf said it was to remind her not to lose that sense of unity. And to recall how she trusted her instincts, without any self-doubt. It was a demonstration of how listening to her instincts can save her life and the ones she loved.

We asked Great Wolf to please take Lynn to her Council of Elders (or her spiritual teachers).

A strong light appeared. It was White Light and it was everywhere. She was in it. As she stepped into it, she noticed there was no shadow. Suddenly she was overwhelmed! The Light came from all directions. It was a White Light collective. This was the spiritual teacher which came forward when we called on her Council. And it was wonderful.

I asked the White Light, "Who is Lynn?"

The answer was immediate. "She's that White Light and she carries great potential energy." We learned about her soul's characteristics of being highly adaptable and being able to become many other things.

She imaged the limitation of time. Yet, in that same moment, she knew that her true self wasn't constrained by time. Lynn could see why it's so important to identify with all creation and its infinity, in order to reduce constraints of limitations that become imposed.

As she contemplated the White Light, it reminded her that this is always with her. By comparison, she could see that not everyone has the White Light strong within them.

Being a Seer, she saw that White Light is her source.

I asked, "What is her soul's life purpose as the White Light?"

The answer came. She's here to spread love. And also she's here to shine her White Light into fears (which she called shadows) in order to bring healing. She explained that the White Light brings the state of consciousness that enables healing to take place.

I asked how she felt about the White Light. Lynn said it encompassed her, held her, was infinite, and caused her to feel loved. It was off the charts! She felt we were just at the tip of the iceberg discovering things about her soul and she wanted more.

She told me that she's a soul that holds unlimited potential and that she can fill roles not yet created. She sees the playing field of infinite possibilities as multiple planes at work, while others insist these things are limited. I felt privileged to be witnessing a vast exposure of what she could do as the unlimited White Light.

She explained that she's a conduit and catalyst for unusual possibilities where things can reach their true potential. As an example, she told me that many of her artist friends consider her a muse because she opens them up. She said, "White Light cannot be contained."

While she'd been talking, I sensed her energy of potentiality. It felt powerful. As I stayed with this sensing, I told her I had an image of her being like a volcano, who was capable of accessing its fire deep within the Earth, and able to bring it up into a fully empowered manifestation into 3-D as it exploded and expanded itself into the atmosphere. I asked if she could relate to that imagery describing her. She said she could.

I asked what would she be like if her fire was turned all the way up?

We had a long conversation about the nature of herself as a soul who carries so much powerful potentiality and manifestation. I could actually feel it the entire time she was talking.

She said that she feels the active volcano within her and sees its flow. She informed me that she barely has to ask before it appears and becomes highly active.

She said that at times it manifests effortlessly and that at this particular time, she's close to being ready to activate her life's potential as she's now ripe.

She feels that her superpower is her potential abundance and, as she steps into her power, it will directly connect her to her abundance.

I named her, "An unstoppable soul where anything good is possible!" She agreed that this is what she carries as a power within her. And she added that the powerful light of love is what determines her destiny with potentiality and its manifestation. Her soul is living a love-directed life.

Towards the end, we asked her question about loved ones who have departed. Lynn wanted to know if they had a message for her.

Each one appeared and conversed with her, including her dad. Her dad apologized for his behavior to her and told her how proud of her he is. This brought tears.

Then she talked with the other deceased friends. These individual encounters brought tears of gratitude as she loosened the burden of grief she'd been carrying for each one of them. It was another outstanding moment of her session.

Lynn shared that the past life revealed how she really holds space for great possibilities and how her intuition was so profoundly right about following her guidance all the way to the northwest mountains, saving herself and her tribe.

And as the tribe had been migrating for so long, she realized that all she had to rely on was her intuition and the *possibility* of finding a new home. These were two powerful innate qualities.

Overall, she felt the regression was confirming and validating of who she is and she was happy to walk away with images to hold of the vibration of being strong and powerful, with a perspective on how the universe provides for her.

She felt closer to her White Light source and to its lovingness. She also felt love from White Light's other aspects of boundlessness, infinity, an all-encompassing presence holding her, and its soothing comfort.

Here's what I observed:

- Lynn told me she first met Great Wolf when she was just a teenager. In a memorable dream she was trapped in a snowstorm late at night and couldn't go home. She decided to burrow herself in a snowbank and this same Great Wolf with very green eyes stayed with her through the night to keep her safe and warm.

- The constant theme of Spirit World Regressions is that you discover who you are as a soul. Also, at this deeper level you can discover your life purpose. This is exactly what Lynn experienced.

- During Lynn's past life, I recalled a few years ago when meeting her for the first time. During our visit, she shared that she loved spending time picking wild herbs, making herbal healing remedies, and even distilling her own essential oils. She told me that she talked with trees and they conversed back. I walked away thinking, "What an amazing Earth woman!" Her past life showed the depth of this.

- Lynn's past life revealed an astounding story that showed her soul's capability of manifesting infinite possibilities. One of the ways she accomplished this was by relying on her inner vision. Seeing was one of her most powerful soulful gifts. Without being a Seer, the possibility of surviving the invasion would have been very dim. From this example, you can see how powerful the quality of *seeing* can be. Her session showed that envisioning and intuition were tremendously evolved within her.

- Always look for clues in past lives in order to better understand your soul's qualities and its gifts. By learning about yourself, you can give yourself credit for the many lessons you've learned and the wisdom you've gained that helps you now.

- Lynn's past life was a powerful example of what can occur from holding possibilities open for ourselves, rather than shutting down and limiting ourselves.

Chapter 14

Strength and Protection from Archangel Michael

Pamela was a smart, young businesswoman in her early 30's, who travels from coast to coast. She was in San Diego during one of her regular business visits and was curious to learn about the mystery of her past lives.

She arrived with the beautiful qualities of openness and curiosity. This was her first regression experience.

I learned during her interview that just prior to her wedding a few years ago, her husband's brother died tragically. He committed suicide. This placed their new marriage in peril with her husband being traumatized and devastated from the loss. In fact, he himself had become suicidal at times. The loss set her husband on a spiritual path to try and find answers.

She expressed needing help for herself because she'd been so engulfed in helping her husband through the traumatic event that she'd lost focus on herself for several years since it began.

Raiders invade

Her past life opened with a scene of herself walking alone along a dirt path in a desert. She was a man who was stranded and had lost something important and was trying to get help.

She arrived at a church where there were steps to the door, but before she could take the first step, she fell down, discovering she'd been shot in the left side of her stomach. Moments later, she rolled onto her back and died, never able to receive help.

We learned more about the traumatic story once she arrived in Spirit World.

I couldn't help but notice that, moments before we began the regression, she had shared her current traumatic story. Now we were visiting another traumatic story only this was in a past life. I wondered what the connection was between the past life trauma and her present trauma.

Spirit World

She arrived in Spirit World and received a healing treatment from a White Light which engulfed her with its warm, expansive vibrations running through her. It felt cleansing.

After that, a different White Light surrounded her with vibrations coming outside of her which felt calming and strong. We spent as much healing time as she needed until Pamela felt cleared of the trauma from the past life.

Her Spirit Guide, Liam, appeared. He exuded strength, safety, and happiness. In his presence she felt strong, safe, and very happy. Liam was wearing a white robe.

Pamela felt an overwhelming sense of love and this is how she recognized him. She compared his deeply nurturing love much like her mom's, which felt unconditional. We paused so she could drink in this love.

We then picked up details of the tragic story of being murdered. Having her Spirit Guide with her to review it was helpful.

Raiders on horses came to steal their cattle and horses. Circling the house, they ambushed them, shot the husband, and then fatally shot the wife and son. Pamela could hear the wife's panicked scream as they entered the house.

Although she made it to the church, she fell and died, completely overwhelmed by the bullet wound and the event of losing her entire family in a tragic way. The loss and state of helplessness were sad as it was too late for help.

Pamela's heartbreak was from not being able to protect her family from the event. Although I wasn't aware of Pamela's emotions as she shared the event with me, she told me later that she had tears as she spoke with me about what happened that day when the raiders arrived, yelling and shooting them in cold blood. (She wasn't sure what year it took place, perhaps in the 1800's.)

Her Spirit Guide, Liam, explained that it was important for her to see the past life because she carried these same feelings into her present life. We listed them as: helplessness, trauma, despair, loneliness, terror, fear, inability to control the situation, overwhelmed, emotionally pained, and desperate to protect her family.

Her guide explained that Pamela carried the quality of powerful protection into her present life and this is what her soul does - it protects, saves, and loves. He told her that she is immensely loving and strong willed and this helps her to be a protector.

I asked her to imagine a mirror in front of her and to describe her appearance. She said she saw white wings that began mid-spine at her shoulder blade and continued down to her hips. She could open her wings and close them as was necessary for responses to protect.

I asked if archangel Michael was present as I knew him to be a protector. She said he was present, and he was her additional guide. I asked to speak with Michael. Michael didn't show himself, at first, but she said she felt him nodding that it was okay for me to speak with him.

I asked what kind of soul she was. Archangel Michael said he was her archetype. I know archangel Michael is known as a powerful protector who carries great divinity in the high Angelic Realm.

Pamela interjected that she's always been unsure as to why, but she always felt a great need to take care of people and to protect them. However, she had a lot of pain from this because she didn't get support in return and she was feeling depleted.

Michael proceeded to help Pamela understand her present life. He explained that, in this life, it will become more balanced. She needs to have patience and keep protecting because the balance had already started. I asked if it had begun with her husband's search for spiritual answers after the loss of his brother. Michael indicated it had.

Michael also shared that he and her Spirit Guide, Liam, were giving her protection and support, helping to balance her life. As a result of her need to over give, she had been neglecting herself for a long time. This resulted in an imbalance.

We paused so that Pamela could take in more help from her guides. From this, she began feeling an overwhelming amount of release, calm, and strength. This was different from the healing she received earlier from the White Light. Now, her guides were restoring her. At completion, she told me she felt "very, very calm and neutral." Her energy of trauma was resolved. I noticed how very calm and soft her lowered voice had become.

I asked archangel Michael how her connection with him originated. It was revealed that she had chosen him after her traumatic past life so that she would be strong and able to help other souls here.

I asked if she was a Spirit Guide and she said that she was in training to become a Spirit Guide. She chose Michael for his role as a protector and because of his immense strength. This was the first incarnation since her tragic past life on the farm. And she had carried the trauma energies into her present life.

As a result of the regression, Pamela's traumas were now cleared.

It was explained that Pamela is part of an Angelic Realm and she came here to connect with her loved ones and assist with their soul purpose. She would be able to do this because of her work as protector and one who loves, which are very powerful qualities.

Michael described her as a soul of love who wants to protect her own life purpose as well.

I asked if Michael could appear to her. Immediately she described his presence of strength. His hands were holding hers. She felt enormous love from him.

As he gently held her hands, archangel Michael told Pamela that she's doing well. She said he kept repeating this.

I asked why she had 2 Spirit Guides. Pamela explained that different ones appear according to the need.

She said Liam had appeared to her before this regression, during a meditation. She recalled feeling his pure love and comfort. She distinguished Michael as her spiritual teacher as well as her protector.

We asked how Pamela can manage help for herself with all the trauma and depression she and her husband have had to live with since the suicide. She explained that she's been trying to protect her husband as well as help him stay on his life path.

Michael explained that she couldn't neglect herself.

She asked if there was a path she needed to be aware of which she didn't know about. He said, "You're on it. Things will reveal themselves over time. You don't need to be overwhelmed."

These were the assurances she needed.

I asked how learning the information from our session would change her. She said that she felt really calm and less anxious than she'd been for a very long time.

She spoke of how overwhelming it had been coming face to face with her soul. She could barely take it all in as it was wonderful to behold.

Pamela shared the additional information that her husband is her soul mate and that he's also a protector soul!

She learned that her husband is also in her Soul Family along with her mother, dad, and brother. They often incarnate together in order to learn lessons they're working on.

Referring to the state of exhaustion Pamela was suffering from when she arrived for the regression, I asked Pamela what percent of her energy she had incarnated from Spirit World.

She answered about 50%. I asked if it was enough and how much did she need for her present life. She said she needed 70%. We then did an exercise where I was able to bring up her energy to 70%. And we acknowledged that if she needed more at times, she could call on her guides and receive all she needed.

As we closed, Pamela exclaimed that she had no previous awareness about any of the things she learned.

Her Spirit World Regression provided a huge awakening and was a life changing event.

She'd always known she was a very protective person. She didn't know that she'd carried over traumatic energies from the past life and was very grateful they were cleared during the session. And that it was good to know she was also protected. She shared that when she first met her husband she felt overwhelmingly protected. I sensed that she and her entire Soul Family are protectors.

Here's what I observed:

- During our interview together, hearing of Pamela's tragic story about her husband's brother's death, I found myself carrying a lot of sadness into the regression session. But as she began receiving much healing in Spirit World and her guides appeared when she began receiving enlightenment about her soul and her soul's path, my heart became very lifted. It touched me.

- There were special moments during Pamela's regression. First, when we learned that she was from the Angelic Realm and archangel Michael was her guide. I had chills learning this. And second, the moment when Michael was holding her hands which was deeply intimate and full of love.

- The past life was brief, but it was loaded with vital information for Pamela in order to clear the trauma energies carried over into her present life. I felt both comfort and relief for her.

- She learned that the wife and child who were murdered in the past life were her present husband and brother, respectively. We shared concern, that perhaps they too had brought in the traumatic energies to their present life. With that awareness she felt compassion.

- It was fascinating information to learn that because of the extreme level of unprotection and vulnerability in her past life that she would begin working with the supreme protector Michael from the Angelic Realm to fulfill her need to become a successful protector herself.

- I knew that all the information she was gaining from the session would change her life forever. She learned that she's from an Angelic Realm and that she has continual access to her Spirit Guide, Liam, as well as archangel Michael. And now that she is aware of this, Pamela can call on them anytime to help her and give her and her loved ones protection.

Chapter 15

My Own Personal Regressions

I've had over 50 Past Life and Spirit World Regressions. Over the course of even the first few regressions, I received extraordinary information about my soul and identity. This is what my hope is for you.

I felt it may be valuable to include some of my own personal experiences that have most shaped me. While everyone is different, as I've studied my regressions, some major themes stand out, and I wanted to share what has been the most meaningful.

A woman alone without love

One past life, I lived alone on the outskirts of a large mass of woods. I was miles and miles away from anything, sometime during the frontier days. I had no real personal relationships and I cooked for groups of workers, about 7 or 8 men for lunch and dinner settings where they came in their work clothes, ate at a picnic size table next to my stove, then left. No words were spoken. They came for food and I was the cook.

My meek log cabin was sparsely furnished with the picnic table, a small bed in the bedroom, and a rocking chair by the window next to the tiny kitchen. The only color anywhere was a lavender colored shawl draped over the rocking chair. There was no explanation for it.

Later, I recalled that a Pony Express rider sometimes came by for food and he gave me this as a gift. It was Scotty, my husband in my present life.

I was not meant to be in a relationship in the past life. In fact, it was revealed to me that I had deliberately chosen this life in order to see what it was like to live a life entirely without love. I chose it out of curiosity. It was a learning experiment. During this life, I lived in contentment but without significant emotion. However, I did enjoy living next to the woods in isolation.

A husband lost at sea

In a second past life, the scene opened where I was on the edge of the sea, having just learned that my husband had been lost at sea. Scotty had again been my husband. It was England in the 1600-1700's.

For the rest of my life, I lived in the little seaport village raising two children, able to earn money by sewing and doing laundry for others. I recall that living by the sea was meaningful to me and its vastness continually felt assuring and supportive. In spite of the great loss of my beloved husband, I lived with peace and independence. I carried contentment deep within me as a life force, as though the sea reminded me of Source as an everlasting presence with me.

Today in this life, we enjoy a home close to the sea!

Almost died but love awaited

In a third past life, I owned a small women's hat shop in London. My shop was located on a main street. I employed young women who worked for me. Once again, I was independent and living well, enjoying keeping my shop. However, I was often harassed and confronted by a crazed man who lived on the streets. One day, he came by the shop yelling accusations to me as though I were the reason that he lived on the streets and was penniless. In spite of his accusations, I didn't know him personally.

One day, he came to find me at the shop. He was enraged and began to attack me, striking me down. As his large body hovered over me and strangled me with the intention of murdering me, I saw the hate in his eyes. It was unforgettable. He looked crazed. I lost consciousness and was given up as dead. Then he left, thinking he had killed me. However, I had only passed out from being strangled.

The next scene opened with me living on a western sea village, far from London. I had closed down my hat shop. Soon after moving there, I met someone and fell in love. We married and lived happily. I had a beautiful death scene where we were holding hands, in the full realization of our great love. All the trauma from the crazed man had vanished into our love, no longer carried in my nervous system nor in my memory.

In this regression, I recognized two men from my present life: the endearing man holding my hand was my husband Scotty, the homeless man who tried to kill me was my ex-husband, to whom I was married for 18 years. We repeated the past life roles in my present life: my ex-husband had also tried to kill me in this life. And once again, when I united with Scotty, the trauma of my ex-husband vanished in our great soul mate love.

Leading parallel lives, one with Jesus

A soul can choose to lead parallel lives where they exist in two separate places at once. This occurred to me during Jesus's time.

During one past life, I emerged as an energy. I learned that I was part of a collective of 2 other soul energies that were gathered to do healing. We were identified as healing energies. We had consciousness, but no body.

The scenes slowly revealed each healing in which I was engaged. One was healing a blind man. Another was healing someone very sick. Another was healing a woman with a bleeding problem. I then realized that these were the healing energies that Jesus utilized in his ministry.

As a healing energy, I felt extreme power and fulfillment, like a high voltage current running at top speed, full of love. I'm familiar with these energies.

Also, during this same time of Jesus, I lived in Southern Italy. I was a female healer, but it wasn't safe to be public about healing, so I did it quietly. People noticed that when they told me about their problems or illnesses, that there was improvement or full healing.

During this time, I heard about a man far away who was doing amazing healing work. His name was Jesus. He taught me remotely his method of healing by using resonance. It was done silently.

Some local women who showed interest in learning how I healed wanted to learn my method. Without a word spoken, we sat in a sewing circle and, as they felt my healing resonance of spiritual energy, they easily picked it up and began offering their healing to others.

We never spoke of healing nor shared any words. This was a time of the Roman Empire. (I recognized one of the women in my healing circle as a good friend from my present life.)

Meeting Mother Mary

These regressions were meaningful to me and in each of these, as I died and crossed over into Spirit World, I was shown my soul strongly aligned with Mary, an archetype of divine Mother Love. This is where the extraordinary occurred.

By having many more Spirit World Regressions, I gained a deeper understanding of my soul identity as Mary. She is my soul's path. I gained a perspective of myself much wider than my present life experience. And, I began to see my spirit identity as the expression of universal love, residing in Source. (Believe me when I say I know how wild this sounds!)

In many subsequent Spirit World Regressions, I found myself residing in Source, the origin of all love. I existed as pure awareness. In Source, I was content, complete, all-knowing, and I felt whole. Beyond this, it's practically indescribable.

From Source, I existed before the world was. I watched the origin moment of first action taking place. Then, I was shown the origin moment of life's first breath taking place. Later, I saw myself shooting out of Source the first time I incarnated. I took Mary with me as an incarnation template. I was astounded over and over by these unimaginable things! During these revelations, I often cried from being so touched by the magnitude of what I was being shown.

There's no coincidence that my occupation in my present life, for over 30 years, has been a spiritual healer who heals with love.

These multiple regressions enabled me to see myself above all these past lives and even the present one, as a presence of universal love, with a much bigger mission than I had imagined. All of these Past Life and Spirit World Regressions were a part of understanding my true self.

Discoveries about Mother Mary in Spirit World

After spending many hours with Mother Mary, and over multiple regressions, here are some things I was shown about Mary. And, each time I was regressed and shown Mary, I viewed various aspects of her. I know she is also available to help you. Here she is:

- Mary is a highly, highly evolved being with her own group of angels helping her.

- She's the Matriarch of all love and she reveals the nature of love as divine.

- Mary represents universal love and she heals from her heart which pours out love through infinite nurturing and caring compassion. She's calming, comforting, giving, guiding, and healing. She mothers all, filling the void in each heart, and she presences unconditional love to each and all. She brings tenderness, sweetness, and she gives birth, birthing love endlessly. Her Presence is all-inspiring and all-encompassing.

- I visited her halo where Source pours out love through her and into the entire universe. Her halo region also contains her host of innumerable angels, messaging her love and helping you to receive it.
- I visited her crown chakra where it's like atomic explosions of love creating and expanding and bellowing outward into the universe at infinite levels, continually and endlessly, covering and permeating all, including yourself.
- I learned that Mary is absolute love, unconditional and divine. Her love is in everything. Whenever she's felt, love awakens.
- As an expander, she also continually expands her capacity of love spanning the universe and beyond. Whenever you're open, you can have the experience of Mary, always available to you, pouring out love to you.
- I became aware that when you say or think, "I'm not loved," you actually prevent yourself from the experience of love, which is always present and available. You must ask for it. Then you become permeated with Her love.
- She wants to become more utilized by you, for you to love others and for you to see how loved and loveable you are and also to see how wonderful you are, completely worthy of love. She shows you that love is a living reality.

- Mary permeates the veil which prevents you from being aware of her and of yourself as a soul of love. Some are sleepers. Others are very close to the light and they're beginning to receive a massive influx of her love. Mary's love may come to you as a presence which fills you. It may come through another person. But you need to recognize it as Love itself. It's always with you. You need not feel desperate for love nor feel the need to grab someone so you can say you're loved. As you realize that you're love itself, out of this awareness, comes love's true experiences.

- In Spirit World, a mirror was held up for me to see myself. I saw Mary. I saw pure love. This is the true template and actualized self of you and of each of us. You are a soul who is coming into awareness of yourself as pure love.

- You've felt her many times. When you've had moments of being deeply loved or feeling deeply loving - a mother or father with their child, a smile filled with warmth and sincerity, a special wish for your personal well-being, a dog wagging a tail or a cat purring in response to you, a person helping you, a kind word or moments when your heart is tenderly touched. Mary is everywhere. You're increasing her on Earth as you become aware of her presence and join her, utilizing her enormous power to make life and living beautiful and love-filled.

- Mary responds as a loving mother to your heartaches. She comes to you in your need for comfort and joy when you need to be pulled out of the dark pit of despair and loneliness. She initiates you to know the feeling of urgency and to respond to the cry of suffering.
- Her angels deliver messages of hope where your spirit may be lifted and your deeper wisdom is derived.
- When turned to, Mary activates love within your body to remember its state of wholeness, and not a state of disease or illness.
- She's the Higher Dimensional Soul Self directing your human self in all ways, and for you to awaken to yourself as divine, whole, and complete as Love.
- Love is Mary's purpose. She creates angels from her love.
- Within her you could place the entire universe - all the galaxies, billions and trillions of star systems, nebulae, spanning infinite light years, and even then there would be more room. She's bigger than all of that, yet she carries all of it with love. She loves and loves and loves and it pours out of her forever.
- She is of Source and also of the Angelic Realm. She is perhaps greater than all the archangels combined. She is truly the unimaginable!
- Mary infuses her powerful love energy, affecting everything and everyone with love,

- which includes you, all the universe, and beyond.
- The universe infuses Mary with all the help, energy, power, intelligence, love, and all that she'll ever need forever. She's magnificently receiving angelic energies, at her powerful vortex which supports you in all ways, especially when you call on her.

Whenever my life becomes difficult or tumultuous, I take a moment to refer back to my true identity and its divine nature, which was revealed to me in Spirit World Regressions as true psychic knowing about myself.

And I'm able to feel sane, grounded, strong, powerful, and ready to go forward. It may not happen instantly, but as I lean on it, it comes more into the realm of my life providing healing. I've relied on this for decades and it leads my life.

A new era of love for Earth

Mary informed me that although the world is in crisis, she showed me how she's presently doing a massive infusion into Earth and into each person, including you.

Mary is engaged in saving Earth and each one of us which requires transforming us at an epic scale. We're engaged in a soul quake, equivalent to a seismic scale of 10,000.

The outcome will affect everyone, creating a new world of love. This is underway and will be realized during most of our lifetimes.

Mary is creating a new culture on Earth which is also affecting the entire universe. In this culture there will be great consideration towards how we affect each other by our words, thoughts, and behavior. We will evolve into a loving culture, although there is presently little sign of it.

It will be a new Age of Love marked by consideration, peace, kindness, tenderness, gentleness, and immense sensitivity in regard to each other. It will change our DNA. Within this culture of love, we will become more evolved and sophisticated with love and we'll know how to express it in every way. We'll invent new ways of loving each other based on our unified oneness. Mary is creating more openings for this to occur now.

As you ask for it, more love comes in. As you look to love, to understand it, more comes in. Make room for love and it will fill you. This is the result of my many regressions, most which have been Spirit World Regressions.

What I've learned as a regressionist

What I've learned as a regressionist is that multiple Past Life and Spirit World Regressions cause you to rise higher and higher into an expanded awareness of your soul's much larger mission which helps to give a new context for your present life predicaments, troubles, and situations which cause you much stress and suffering.

The larger picture of who you are takes precedence over the smaller and overrides it by using your soul's perspective. Your soul's reality is beyond magnificent!

In advanced regressions, what you learn about yourself can be mind-blowing. I've seen with many clients that what seems extraordinary and even unbelievable is that your soul is always pointing to a higher true selfhood of you as a soul. And this overrides the human self and becomes very clear that you're primarily a soul who is having a human experience. This is a truly awakening experience.

For me, there's no greater awakening in life than to know yourself in soul.

It not only fulfills what's deep within your heart (perhaps so buried that it's unknown to you, but you'll recognize it when you see it), but it also helps guide your present life from a perspective that creates maximum possible healing and expansion with life purpose and of becoming even more of who you naturally are.

This brings me to a vitally important point for you to recall after you experience a regression.

No matter what your present life situation is, or how difficult the circumstances or people seem to be, or how impossible it appears, the moment you pull away from your present story to a higher place to recall the beauty of your soul and all the revelations you've been shown, the more this takes over your entire life and begins to transform your present situation.

And by doing this over time, it is truly life changing beyond words.

I began this book by speaking about the importance of how you identify yourself.

You are truly a spiritual being having a human experience. The more you identify with your soul, and allow it to have expression in your life, the more deeply fulfilled and at peace you will become, even lessening your fear of death as you realize that who you are is eternal, and that your soul was never born and can never die.

Your passions live on with you, and anchor you in Spirit World, and regression is a way to tap into that Source and receive all the nourishment, direction, guidance, and reassurance you need on your path.

May your soul be blessed in every way!

About the Author

Shannon Peck is a certified Past Life Regression and Spirit World Regression counselor. She utilizes Past Life and Spirit World Regression as a powerful tool to help clients discover their identity as a soul, their life purpose, and to find healing.

As an interfaith minister, she has been a spiritual healer for over 30 years. Known as a "Love Healer," her work is centered on the healing power of divine Love.

She is also a certified Usui Holy Fire III Reiki Master Teacher and often utilizes Reiki healing energy during regression sessions.

Shannon has a global practice spanning U.S., U.K., Canada, France, Greece, Italy, Australia, Mexico, and Japan. She lives in sunny San Diego with her soul mate husband, Scotty.

For lots of love and healing, visit

www.ShannonPeck.com

Contact or Book a Session with Shannon

I'd love to hear from you! To contact me with questions or to book a regression, you can reach me at:

ShannonPeck@gmail.com

A free gift and more information is waiting for you at:

www.ShannonPeck.com

I look forward to hearing from you.

Love,

Shannon

Printed in Great Britain
by Amazon